THIS BOOK BELONGS TO:

Miria Oshima ♡

All rights reserved. Published by Graphix, an imprint of Scholastic Inc.,
Publishers since 1920. SCHOLASTIC, GRAPHIX, and associated logos are
trademarks and/or registered trademarks of Scholastic Inc.

The publisher does not have any control over and does not assume any
responsibility for author or third-party websites or their content.

Library of Congress Control Number: 2018953575

ISBN 978-1-338-35384-6

10 9 8 7 6 5 4 3 2 1   19 20 21 22 23

Printed in China   62
First edition, May 2019
Edited by Cassandra Pelham Fulton
Book design by Phil Falco
Color by Stephanie Yue, Gurihiru, and Braden Lamb
Lettering by John Green and Jenny Staley
Author photo by Joseph Fanvu
Publisher: David Saylor

Share Your Smile

Your

Raina's Guide to Telling Your Own Story

Raina Telgemeier

graphix

An Imprint of

SCHOLASTIC

WELCOME

Hi! Raina Telgemeier here. Welcome to *Share Your Smile*. I've been journaling and drawing comics since I was a kid, and I've published several graphic novels – some about my own true stories, and some about stories I imagined. Interested in telling your own stories and making them come to life? Let's use this journal to work together!

My graphic memoirs, *Smile* and *Sisters*, are true stories about my life, family, friends (and frenemies), and what it was like growing up in San Francisco. *Smile* centers on the dental drama that followed after an accident, and *Sisters* is about an eventful road trip I took with my family!

I've also created fiction, such as *Drama*, which was inspired by my time as part of the theater programs in my middle school and high school, and *Ghosts*, which was inspired by the atmospheric towns of Northern California.

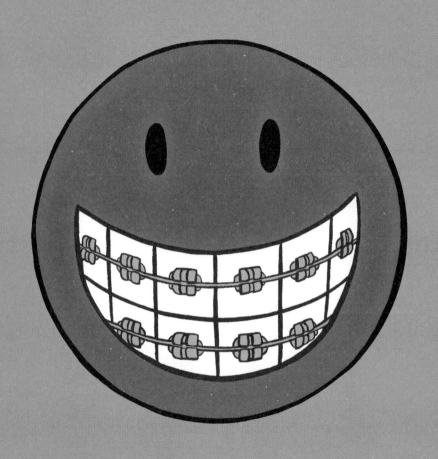

CHAPTER 1
SHARE YOUR SMILE

AN EXCERPT FROM SMILE

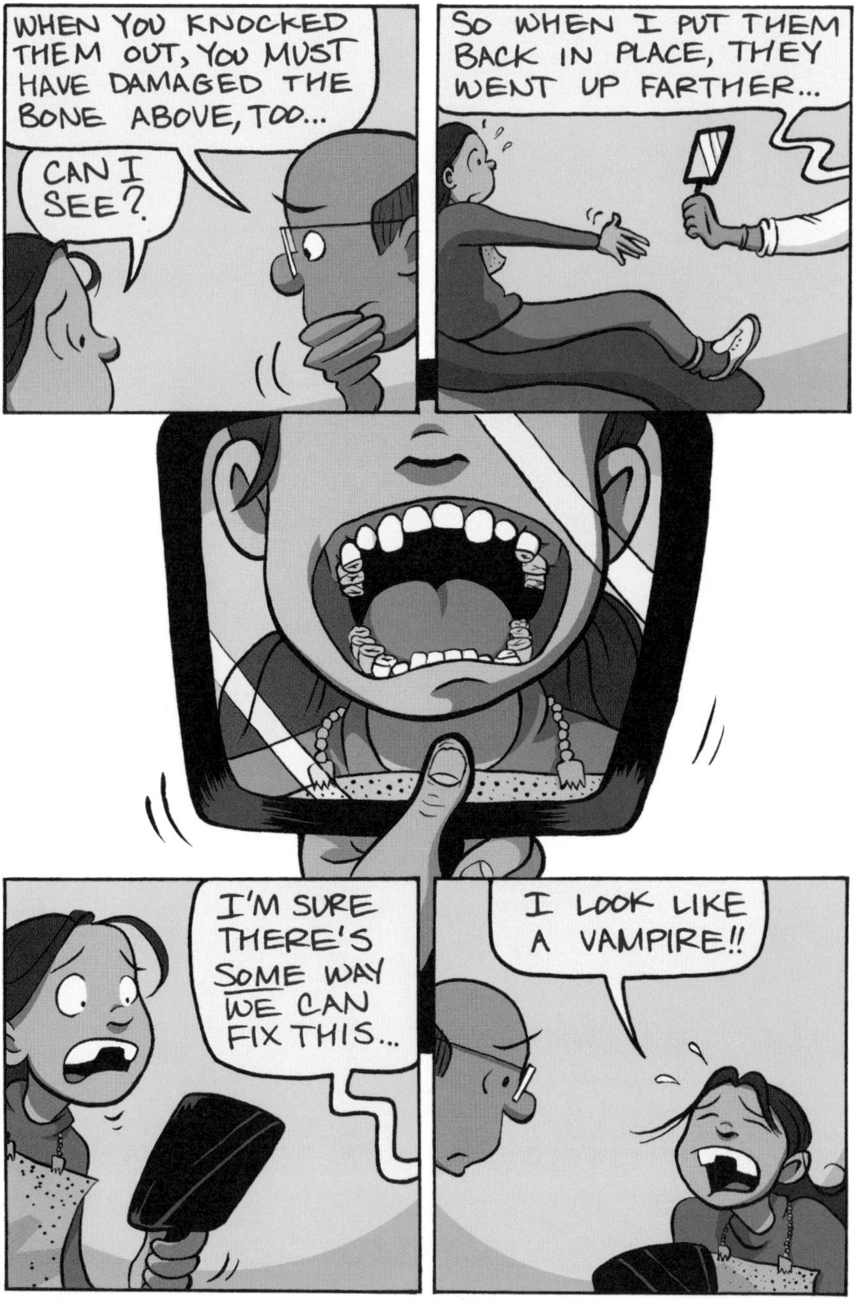
WHEN YOU KNOCKED THEM OUT, YOU MUST HAVE DAMAGED THE BONE ABOVE, TOO...
CAN I SEE?
SO WHEN I PUT THEM BACK IN PLACE, THEY WENT UP FARTHER...
I'M SURE THERE'S SOME WAY WE CAN FIX THIS...
I LOOK LIKE A VAMPIRE!!

LET'S LOOK AT YOUR X-RAYS...

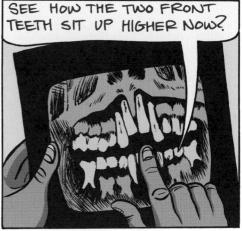

SEE HOW THE TWO FRONT TEETH SIT UP HIGHER NOW?

CAN YOU BRING HER FAMILY BACK HERE?

SURE.

...LOOKS LIKE THERE'S SOME NERVE DAMAGE TO THE FRONT FOUR...

LEMME SEE?

...TO AN ENDODONTIST FOR ROOT CANALS...

C'MON, SIS!

OKAY...

...TRY TO SAVE THOSE TEETH, SO SHE'S NOT WEARING DENTURES AT ELEVEN YEARS OLD...

HA HA HA!

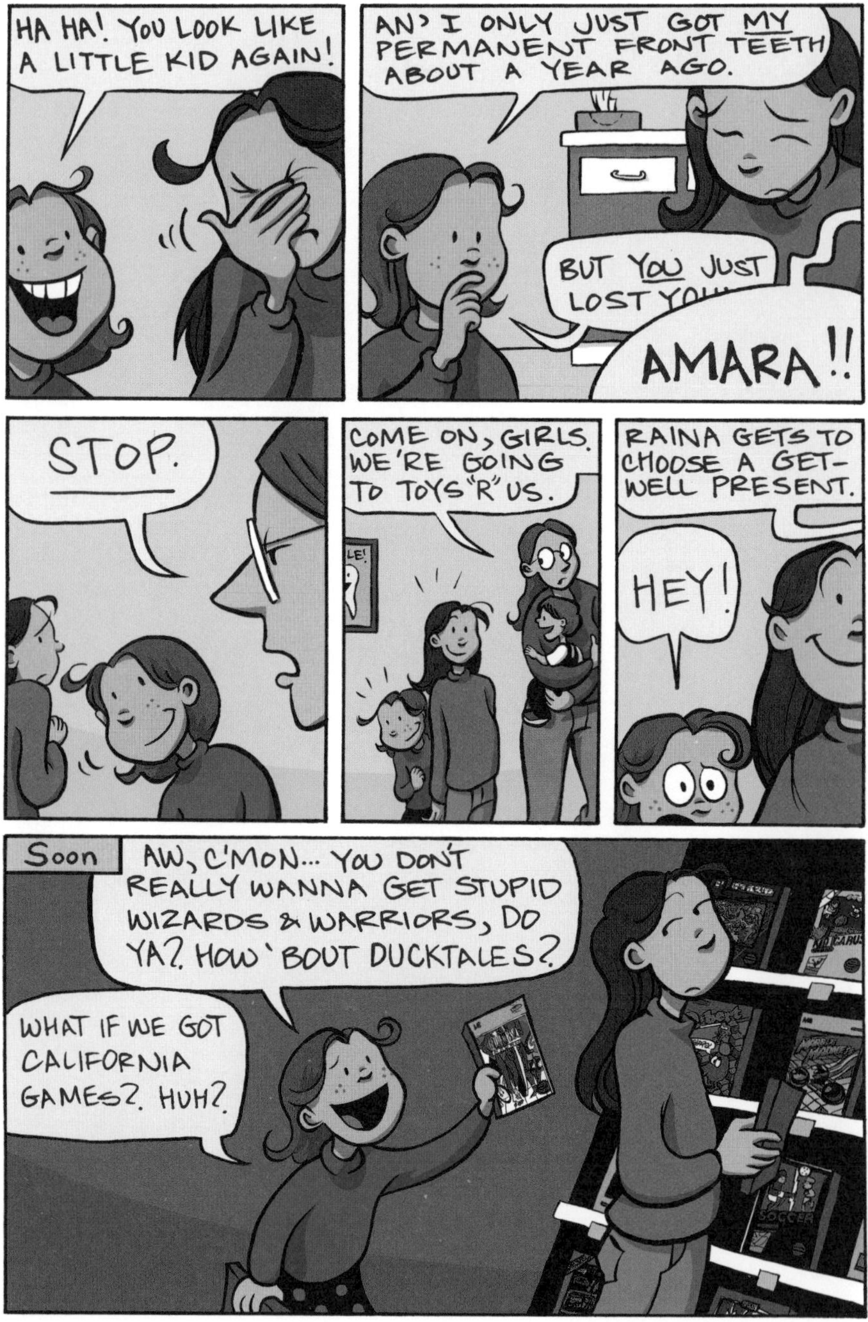
HA HA! YOU LOOK LIKE A LITTLE KID AGAIN!
AN' I ONLY JUST GOT MY PERMANENT FRONT TEETH ABOUT A YEAR AGO.
BUT YOU JUST LOST
AMARA!!
STOP.
COME ON, GIRLS. WE'RE GOING TO TOYS "R" US.
RAINA GETS TO CHOOSE A GET-WELL PRESENT.
HEY!
Soon
AW, C'MON... YOU DON'T REALLY WANNA GET STUPID WIZARDS & WARRIORS, DO YA? HOW 'BOUT DUCKTALES?
WHAT IF WE GOT CALIFORNIA GAMES? HUH?

Each book is different, but they're all influenced by some aspect of my real-life experiences. I'm often asked about what it takes to create a graphic novel, and the truth is, most of what it takes is time, dedication, and a desire to tell a story! (And, you know, lots and lots and lots of practice.)

In this book, you'll find all of my tips, tricks, and inspirational kick-starters for getting your story down on paper. I'll also give you sneak peeks into the cool behind-the-scenes stuff that went on while creating my own graphic novels. Whether you're just interested in learning more about my creative process, or you're all-out ready to create your own graphic novel (woo-hoo!), I can promise you one thing: By the end of this book, you'll definitely be ready to make others smile with *your* personal story.

Raina

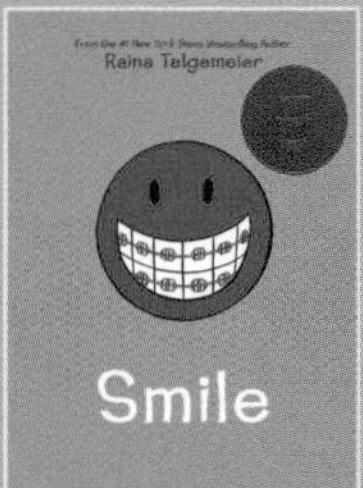
Raina Telgemeier
Smile
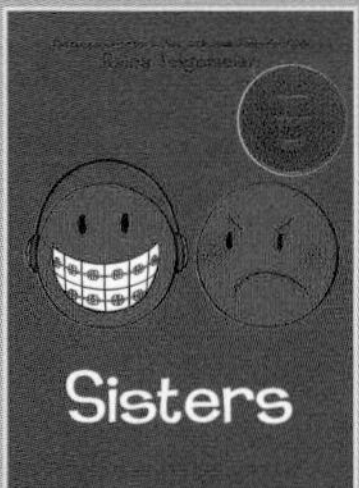
Sisters
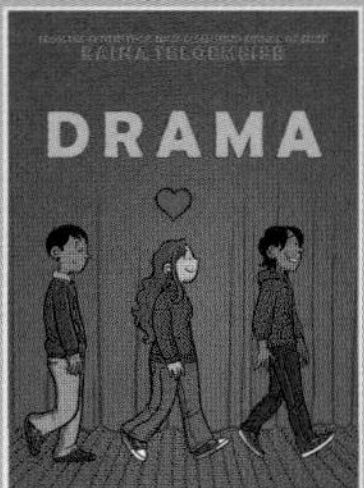
DRAMA
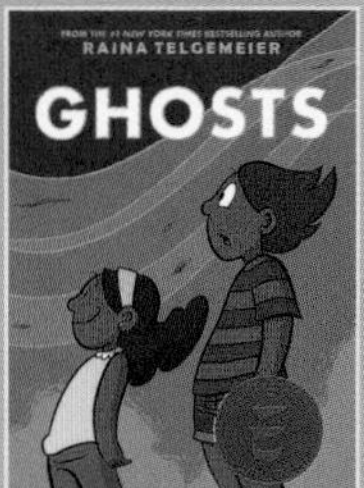
RAINA TELGEMEIER
GHOSTS

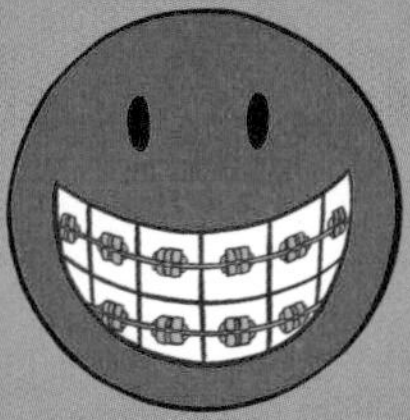

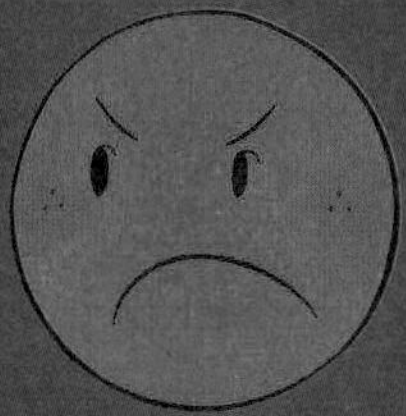

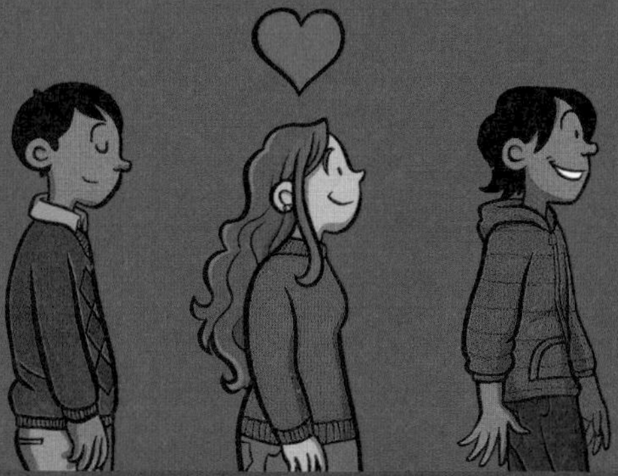

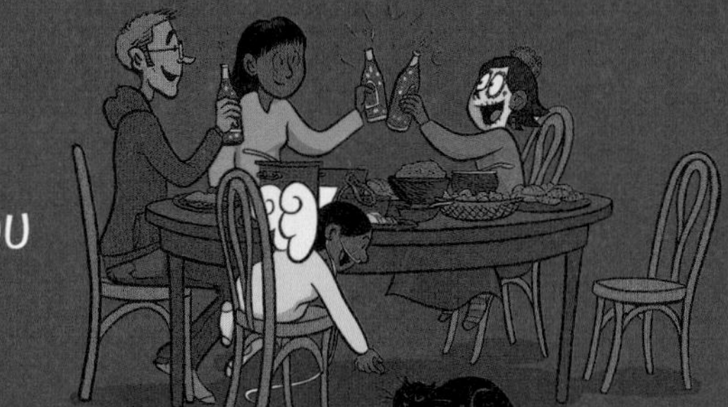

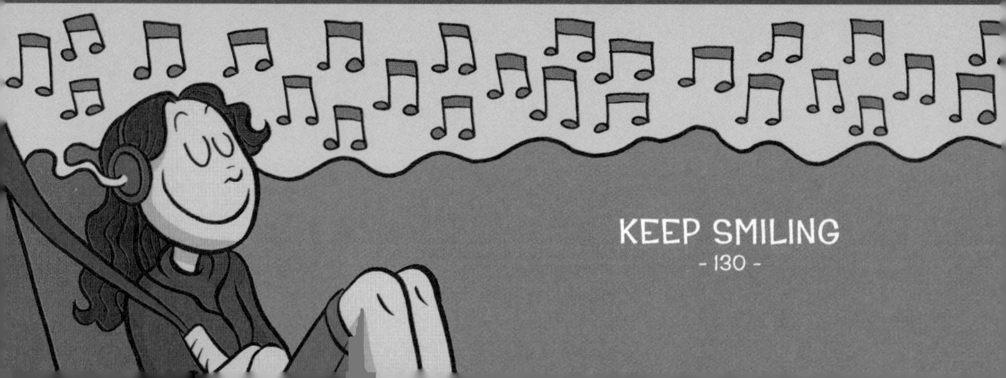

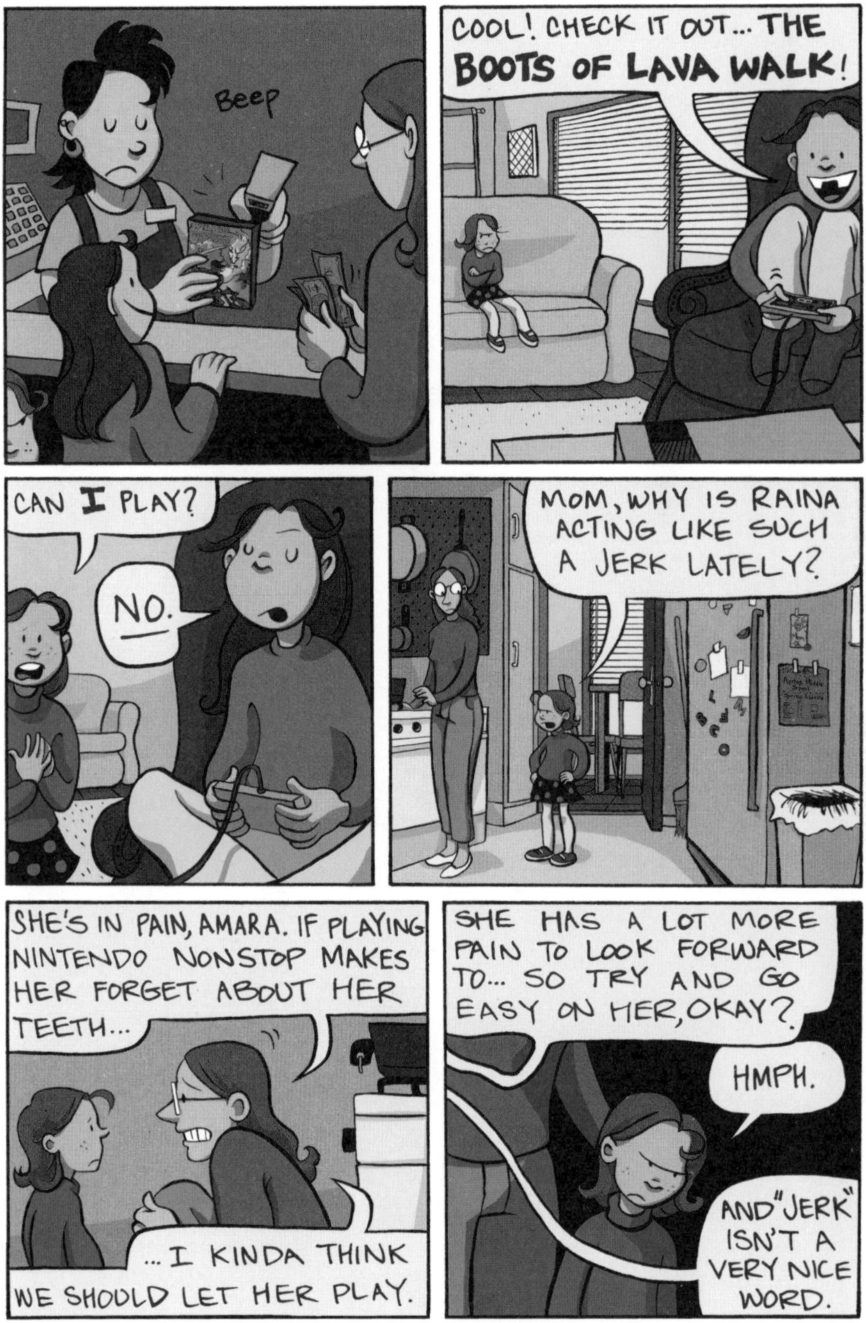
Beep
COOL! CHECK IT OUT... THE BOOTS OF LAVA WALK!
CAN I PLAY?
NO.
MOM, WHY IS RAINA ACTING LIKE SUCH A JERK LATELY?
SHE'S IN PAIN, AMARA. IF PLAYING NINTENDO NONSTOP MAKES HER FORGET ABOUT HER TEETH...
...I KINDA THINK WE SHOULD LET HER PLAY.
SHE HAS A LOT MORE PAIN TO LOOK FORWARD TO... SO TRY AND GO EASY ON HER, OKAY?
HMPH.
AND "JERK" ISN'T A VERY NICE WORD.

ABOUT Smile

When I was eleven years old, I fell on my way home from Girl Scouts and knocked out my two front teeth. The dentist was able to put them back in, but they wound up sitting higher in my mouth than before – making me look like a vampire! I had to undergo root canals, headgear, and braces, all to discover that those two front teeth just wouldn't go back to their original places. So, my orthodontist came up with a revolutionary idea: They would extract my two front teeth (again) and use braces to bring the rest of my top teeth closer together to make my smile look (hopefully) normal. It would require years of orthodontic work, some experimental dentistry, and lots of awkward school photos. Oh – did I mention all this was happening during middle school and high school? Fun times!

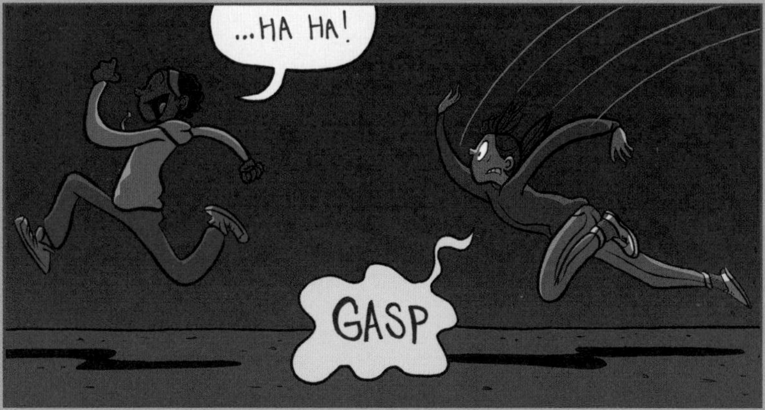
...HA HA!
GASP

I've been telling people about what happened to my teeth ever since sixth grade. The story had plenty of strange twists and turns, and I found myself saying, "Wait, it gets worse!" a lot. Eventually, I realized I really needed to get it all down on paper. I had been writing short-story comics for several years, and my tooth tale seemed like a good candidate for a longer narrative comic.

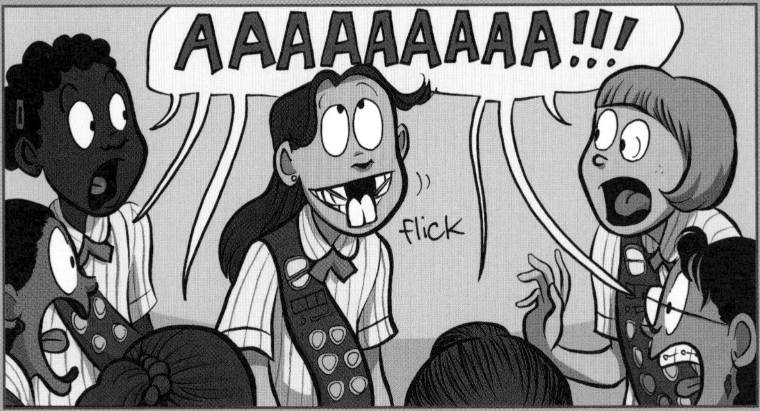
AAAAAAAAA!!!
flick

As I wrote and drew the story, I was able to look back and actually laugh at some of my more painful experiences. What I went through with my teeth wasn't fun, but I lived to tell the tale and came out of it a stronger person. The process of creating *Smile* was therapeutic for me, and put me in touch with many kindred spirits.

I hope my story helps inspire you to share yours! Keep reading if you'd like to know how I created *Smile* before trying your hand at telling your own story!

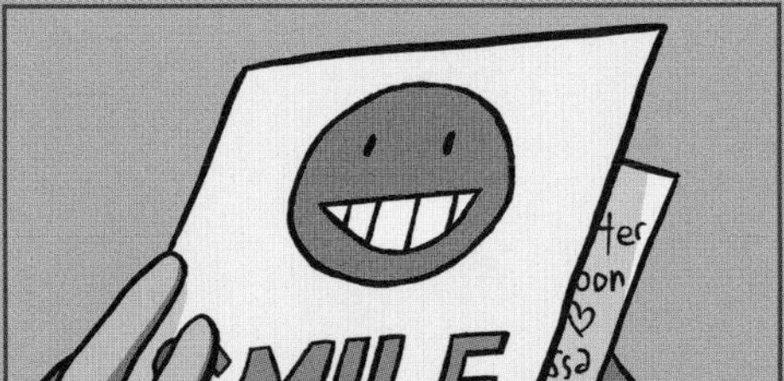
SMILE
wishes
better, Tony

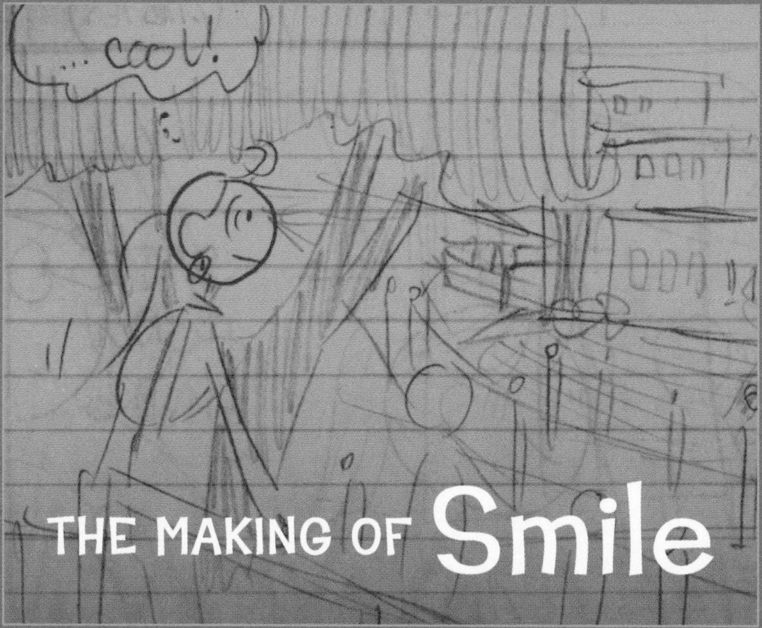
... cool!

THE MAKING OF *Smile*

Because I started working on *Smile* as a personal project long before it was published by Scholastic/Graphix, my methods of working were pretty loose, and I did not document every stage of my creative process very well! But the following steps are, essentially, what went into the making of this book.

STEP 1: IDEA BUILDING

Smile is based on real events in my life, but almost twenty years passed before I felt ready to commit those memories to paper. A few years before I began writing and drawing pages, I jotted down some of my ideas and memories as a list, just to remind myself of the order in which everything happened. (Most of my books start out with a similarly vague form of brainstorming!) I updated, expanded, and revised this list as I went along, but for the most part, I knew where the story was headed and all the major plot points I wanted to include.

STEP 2: THUMBNAILS

Eventually, I felt ready to dive in and tell my story. The title "Smile" came to me before I began writing or drawing, and it seemed a fittingly ironic title for the awkwardness I knew the story would encompass.

First, I sketched out all the pages as thumbnails in a lined notebook. Thumbnails are the format that I write in – I loosely sketch out both words and pictures in a notebook, to make sure my ideas flow visually. Some cartoonists start with a written, text-only script, but I find it easier to get my thoughts out of my head this way.

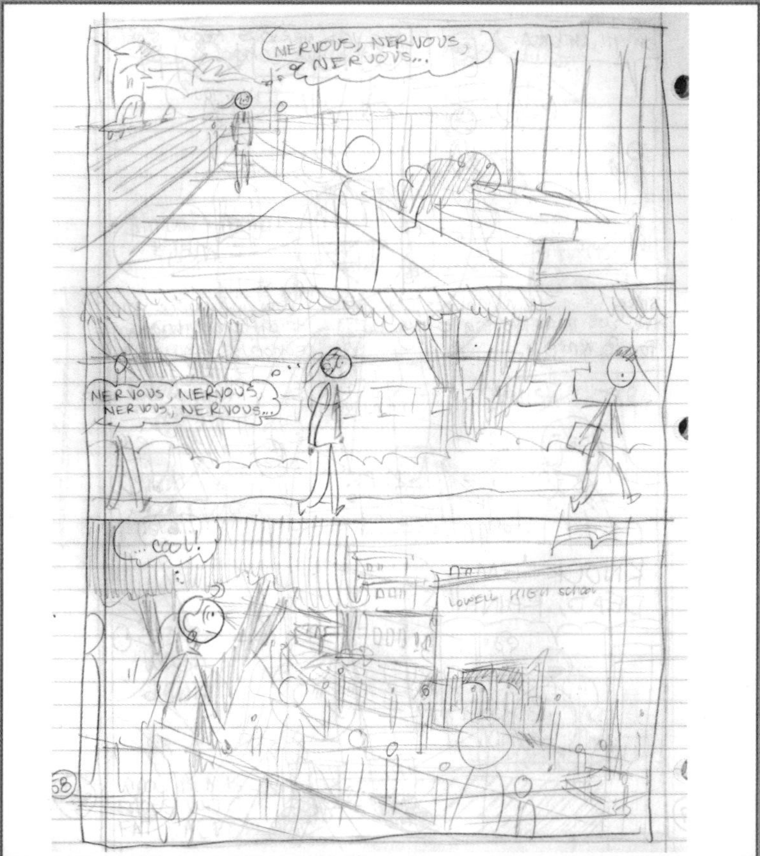
NERVOUS, NERVOUS, NERVOUS...
NERVOUS, NERVOUS, NERVOUS, NERVOUS...
...COOL!
58

STEP 3: PENCILS

On a fresh piece of 9" x 12" Bristol board, I resketched my loose layouts (including the word balloons and dialogue) with a blue colored pencil, then went over those with a mechanical No. 2 pencil to tighten up the artwork. I spend more time at this stage than any other, making sure everything fits into the panels and flows just how I want it to. I do a lot of erasing and redrawing!

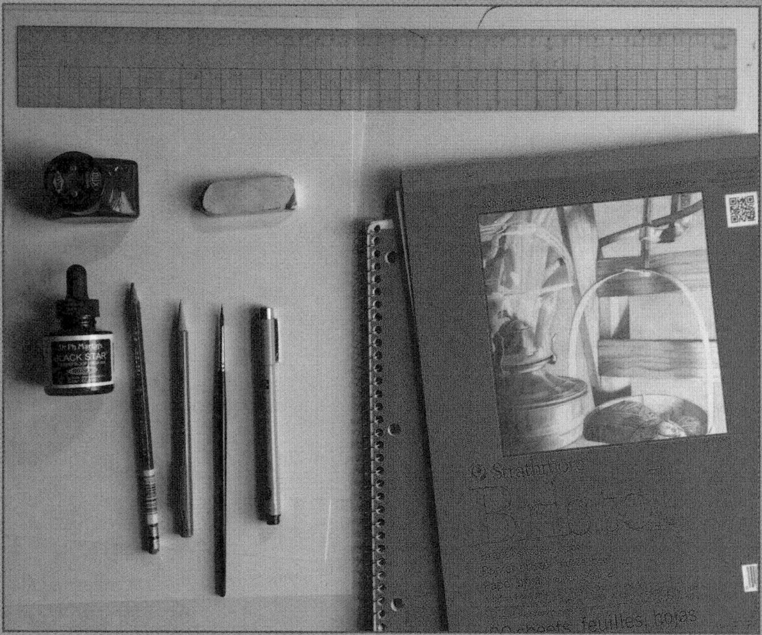
BLACK STAR
Strathmore

STEP 4: PANEL BORDERS, WORD BALLOONS, AND DIALOGUE

Using a 0.8 Pigma Micron pen and a clear gridded plastic ruler, I traced all the panel borders and word balloons in ink, and, using the same pen, added all the dialogue and sound effects by hand. *Smile* is the only comic I've ever lettered by hand – all my other books have been lettered digitally, using a font based on my handwriting. I love the way hand lettering looks, but it was the hardest thing for me to keep neat and steady, and it made my wrist very sore!

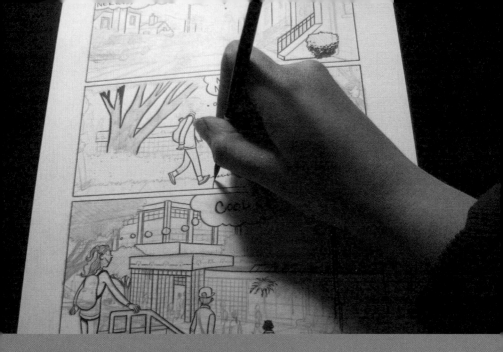

STEP 5: INKING

This is my favorite stage of the comic-making process. Almost all my inking is done with a #2 Winsor & Newton Series 7 Kolinsky sable watercolor brush, dipped in black waterproof India ink (my favorite is Dr. Martin's Black Star HiCarb ink). I inked right over my pencil art, essentially tracing the lines I drew in the last step. Brushes are great because you can create both thick and thin lines with the same tool. There are always a few little details on each page that are easier to ink with a pen than a brush, so I save those for last: things like eyeballs, braces on teeth, and buttons on people's shirts.

STEP 6: DIGITIZING

After I finished the inks, I erased all the pencil lines and scanned the pages into the computer. I used the scanner's line art setting at 600 dpi (dots per inch), so I'd have nice crisp line art to work with. I cleaned up all my stray lines in Photoshop, which means that occasionally my original art is a little messier than what you see on the printed page. But not by much!

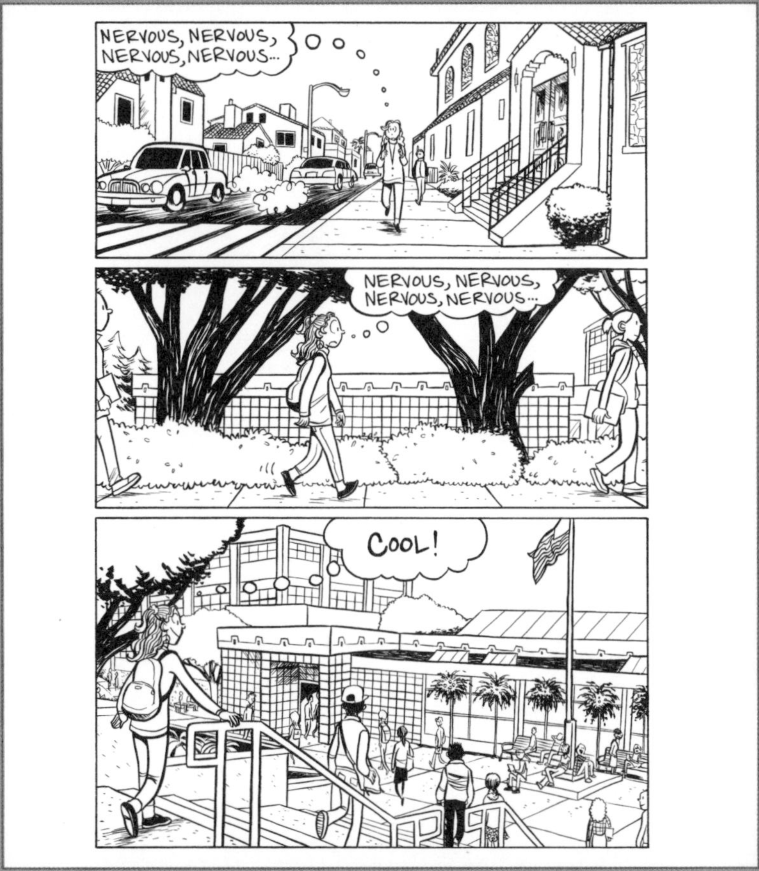
NERVOUS, NERVOUS,
NERVOUS, NERVOUS...
NERVOUS, NERVOUS,
NERVOUS, NERVOUS...
COOL!

Back when *Smile* was a black-and-white webcomic, this was my final step! I converted the image to grayscale, sized the page file down to 72 dpi, saved it as a JPEG, and then uploaded it onto the Web, one page per week, for several years. People read the story as I was writing it, and it was really fun to receive feedback from my readers every time I posted something new!

STEP 7: COLOR

I had been creating *Smile* as a webcomic for about three years when Scholastic offered to publish it as a book. At that point, working on

Smile became my full-time job! I wrote, drew, and inked the final eighty or so pages of the story (plus, I very lightly edited and revised parts of the book I had already finished) in about nine months. Meanwhile, the first 120 pages were sent off to my colorist, Stephanie Yue. Steph looked at some reference photos of my home and neighborhood and asked me a few questions about what colors I liked (and didn't like) wearing when I was a tween, and got to work! She really did a fantastic job of establishing the color palette for the story, and all the stories about my life that would come after *Smile*.

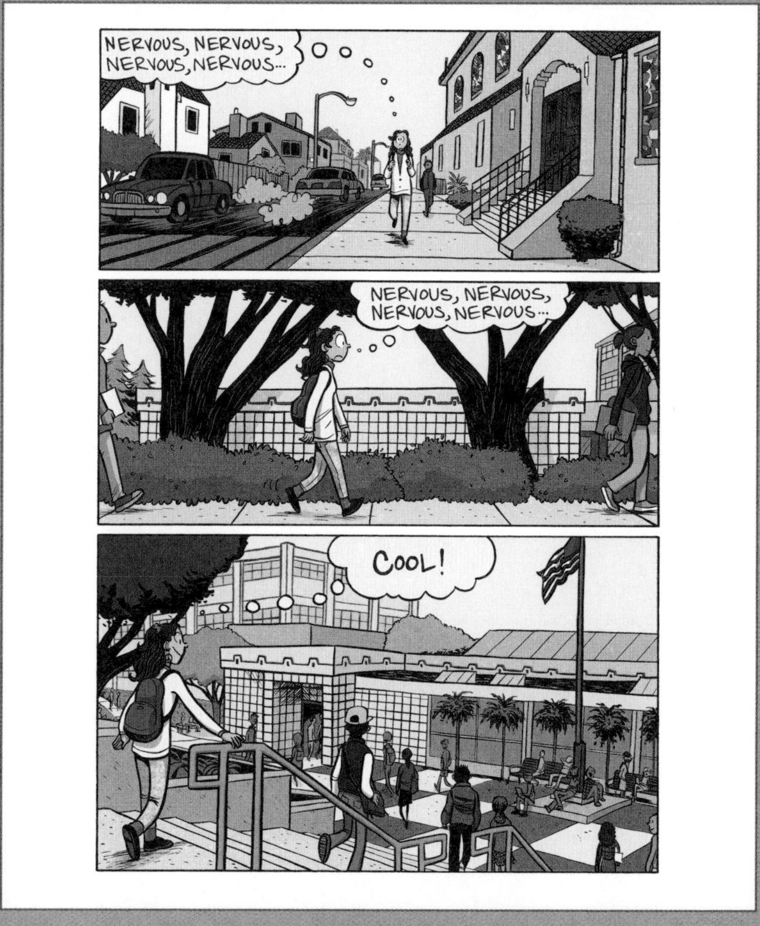
NERVOUS, NERVOUS, NERVOUS, NERVOUS...
NERVOUS, NERVOUS, NERVOUS, NERVOUS...
COOL!

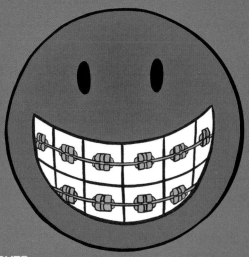

STEP 8: COVER

The cover went through a LOT of changes before we settled on the design everyone now knows and loves! Here are a few of the early versions we considered.

Smile
A DENTAL DRAMA
BY
RAINA TELGEMEIER

SMILE
Raina Telgemeier

raina telgemeier
Smile
a true story

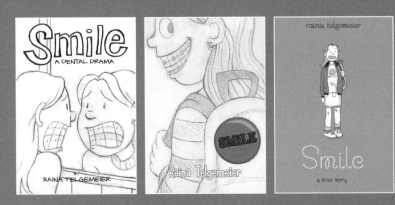

I really wanted the character (me!) to appear on the cover, but the Graphix creative team had the good intuition to use something a little more iconic. Even though it looks very polished, I created the artwork by hand, including the lines that represented the braces. These lines were then swapped out for silver foil at the book's printer.

I hope you enjoyed this peek into the making of *Smile*!

ARE YOU READY TO SHARE YOUR STORY?

Smile started out as a story I told friends and family over and over until I decided to turn it into a book that I could share with the world.

What personal stories are important to you? Do you have funny family memories you love to tell time and again? Or perhaps an experience that changed your perspective on things and made you the person you are today?

These next few pages will help you think about how to start sharing your story the way only you can. Because, after all, the author of your story is you!

ALL ABOUT YOU

What's your name?

Miria

Where do you live?

Kelton ave. 2357

Have you ever lived anywhere else? If so, where?

S. Bentley ave. 1726

What grade are you in?

3rd grade

Who's in your family?

Dad, mom, brother

What three words describe you best?

Talented, Smart, Nice

What are some of your favorite things to do?

Basketball & Art

What are your unique talents?

Gymnastics, Hula hooping
Art, Basketball, Reading

Who are your friends? What do you enjoy most
about hanging out with them?

Zalie and Maya and
Eva hang out and

Describe a time when you felt really proud.

Yesterday

If you feel scared or embarrassed, how do
you make yourself feel better?

tell my friend

What's your favorite childhood memory?

Doing reflexes

What was the worst accident you ever had? How long did it
take you to get better, and what did you need to do?

Bust my lip 1 month
or so.

Write down a funny family story that you like to share over and over.

Santa Barbara

sometimes
play

A PICTURE IS WORTH A THOUSAND WORDS

I created *Smile* entirely from memory, and really dug deep into my family photo albums for inspiration. Take a look at some of my personal snapshots that helped create the artwork for *Smile*.

Seventh grade. I was trying so hard to look cool.

Eighth grade, when my hair decided it was wavy instead of straight. At this point, I had full braces again, and the fake teeth were wired in place while my gap closed. No more retainer, and people really couldn't tell my teeth were "different" anymore. That was fine with me.

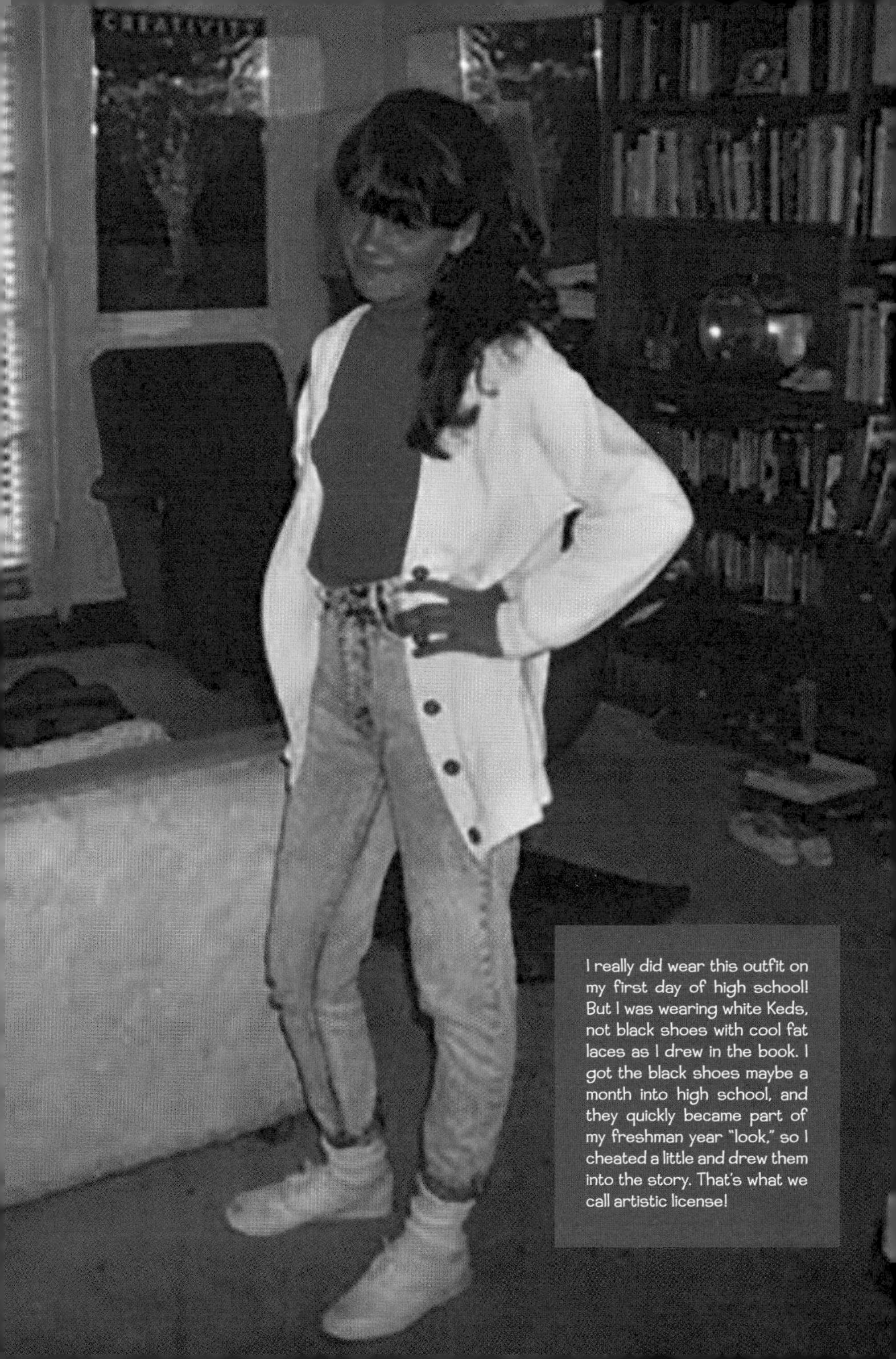
CREATIVITY

I really did wear this outfit on my first day of high school! But I was wearing white Keds, not black shoes with cool fat laces as I drew in the book. I got the black shoes maybe a month into high school, and they quickly became part of my freshman year "look," so I cheated a little and drew them into the story. That's what we call artistic license!

YOUR PHOTO ALBUM

Use these pages to paste pictures of yourself, your family and friends, or anything that you enjoy! (If you only have digital photos, ask an adult to help you print them.) Don't forget to share a caption underneath each about what makes them a special part of your personal story.

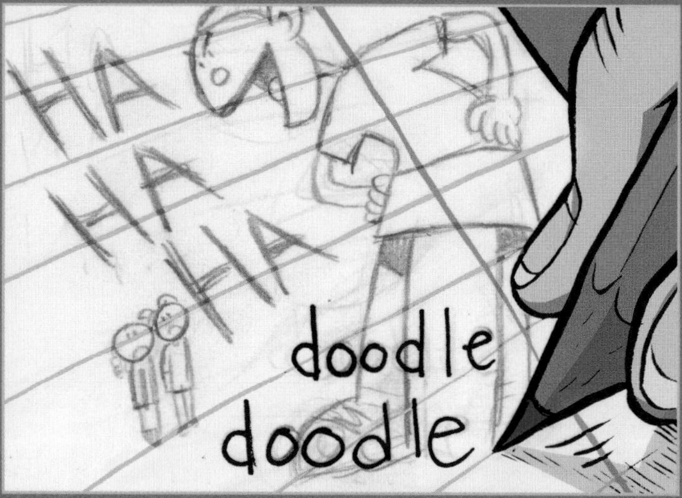
HA
HA
HA
doodle
doodle

LET'S GET DRAWING

Drawing comics takes a lot of patience and a *lot* of practice. But it always starts with a character. Follow my easy steps to practice character drawing, and then try your hand at drawing your own family and friends on the next pages.

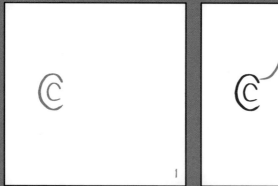

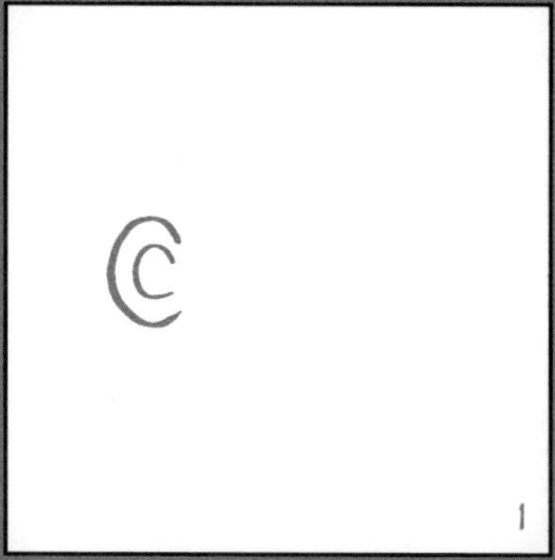
1

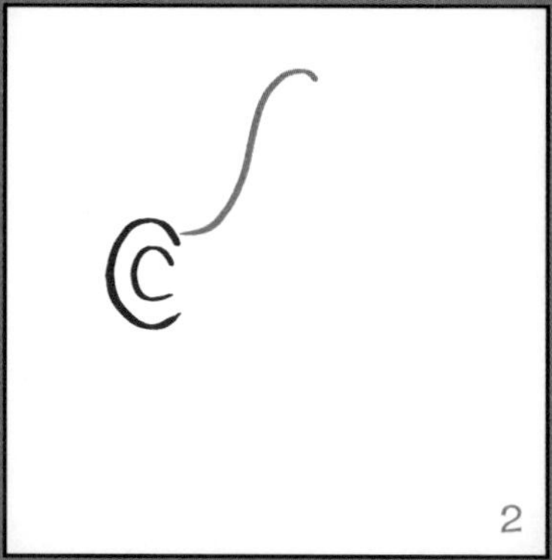
2

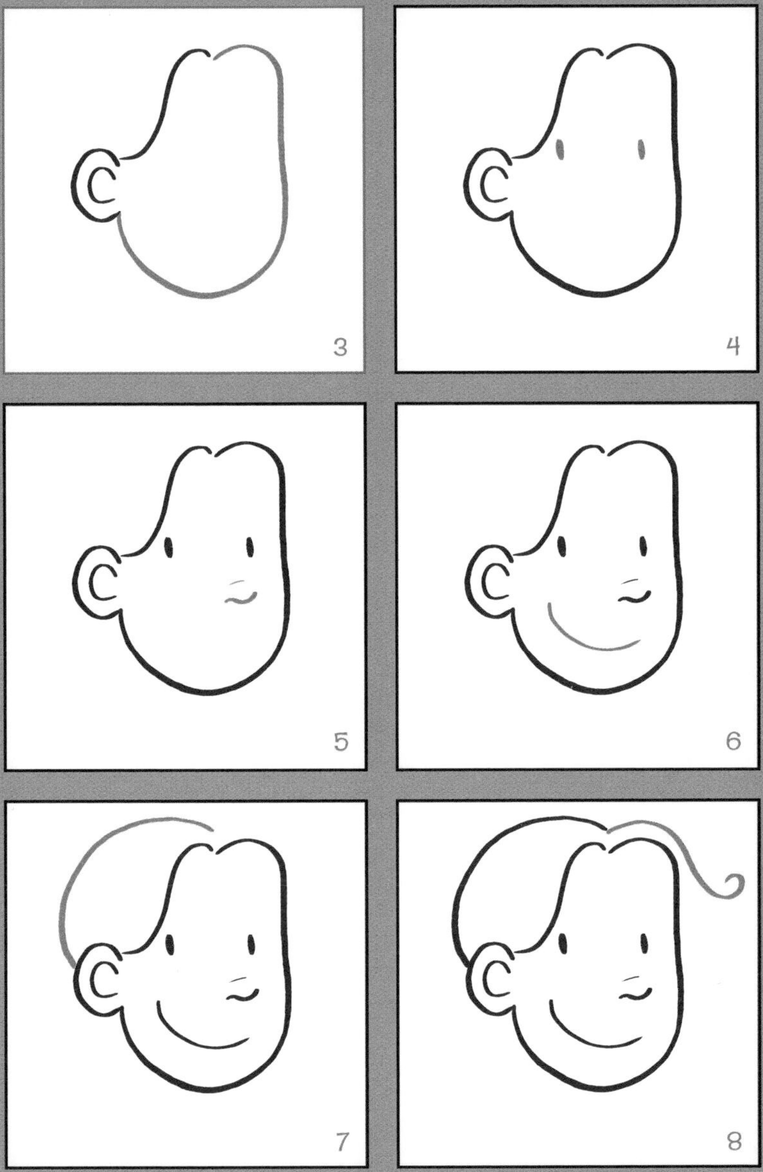
3
4
5
6
7
8

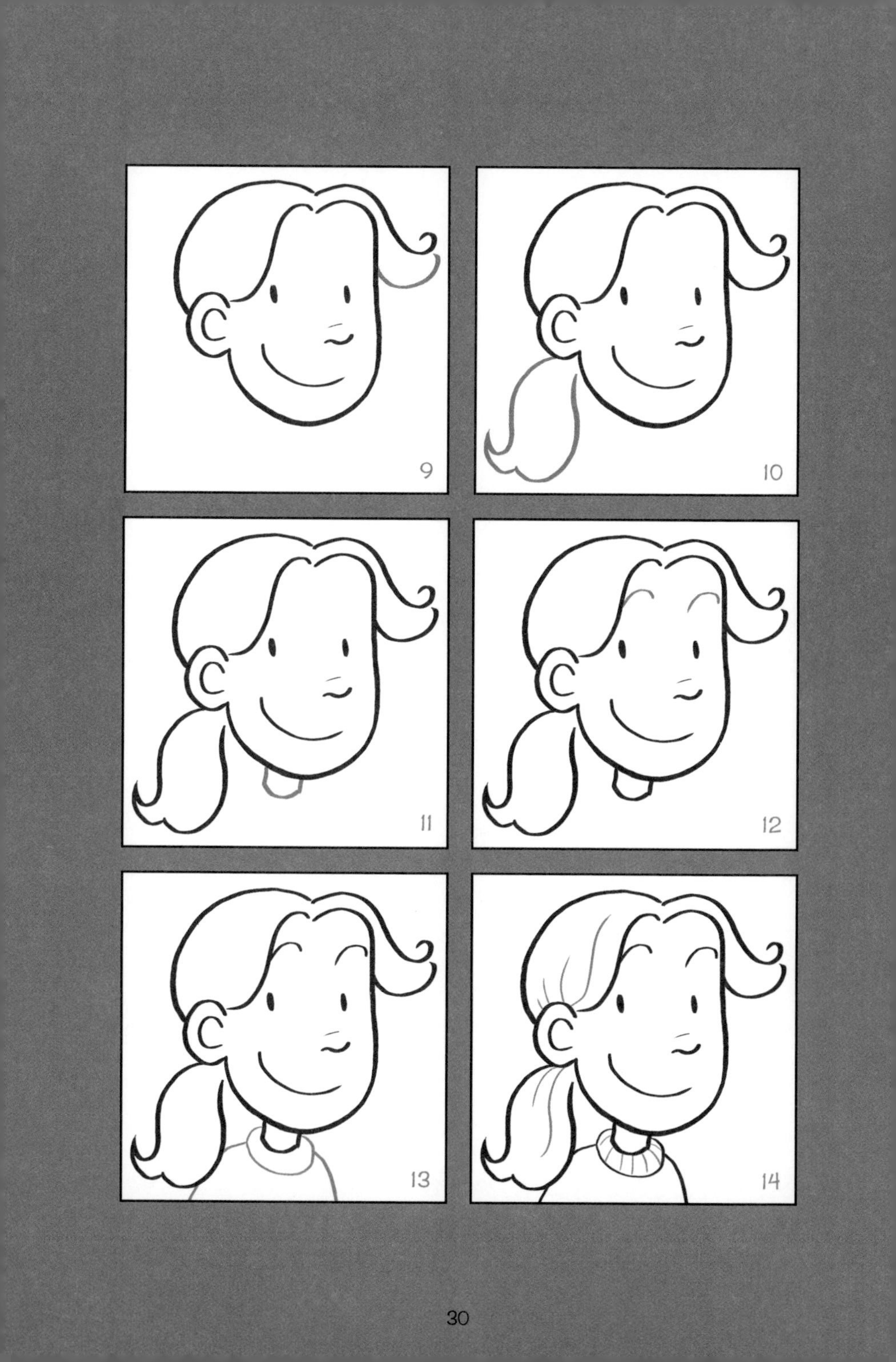
9
10
11
12
13
14

DRAW YOUR FAMILY AND FRIENDS

Now practice drawing your family and friends in the spaces on these pages. Don't forget to draw yourself, too. You can draw your characters as animals, superheroes, or even shapes – anything you enjoy drawing!

Draw lightly with pencil at first so it's easy to erase unwanted lines. When you're happy with your drawing, then trace over it in ink.

TIP Don't worry if your drawing doesn't come out right the first time. Just keep at it. It took years for me to develop my drawing style - and I'm still trying to improve!

TIP

Start with loose shapes
to define the character's
proportions and pose.

WHAT'S IN A FACE?

Facial expressions can change the entire mood of a panel, a page, or even the whole story. I've used hundreds of different facial expressions for my characters in order to show their emotions and reactions. Check out these examples!

HAPPY
Big grin; high, arched eyebrows

SURPRISED
Open-mouth smile showing tongue; wide-set, arched eyebrows

PAIN
Squiggly eyebrows; extra shock lines in eyes

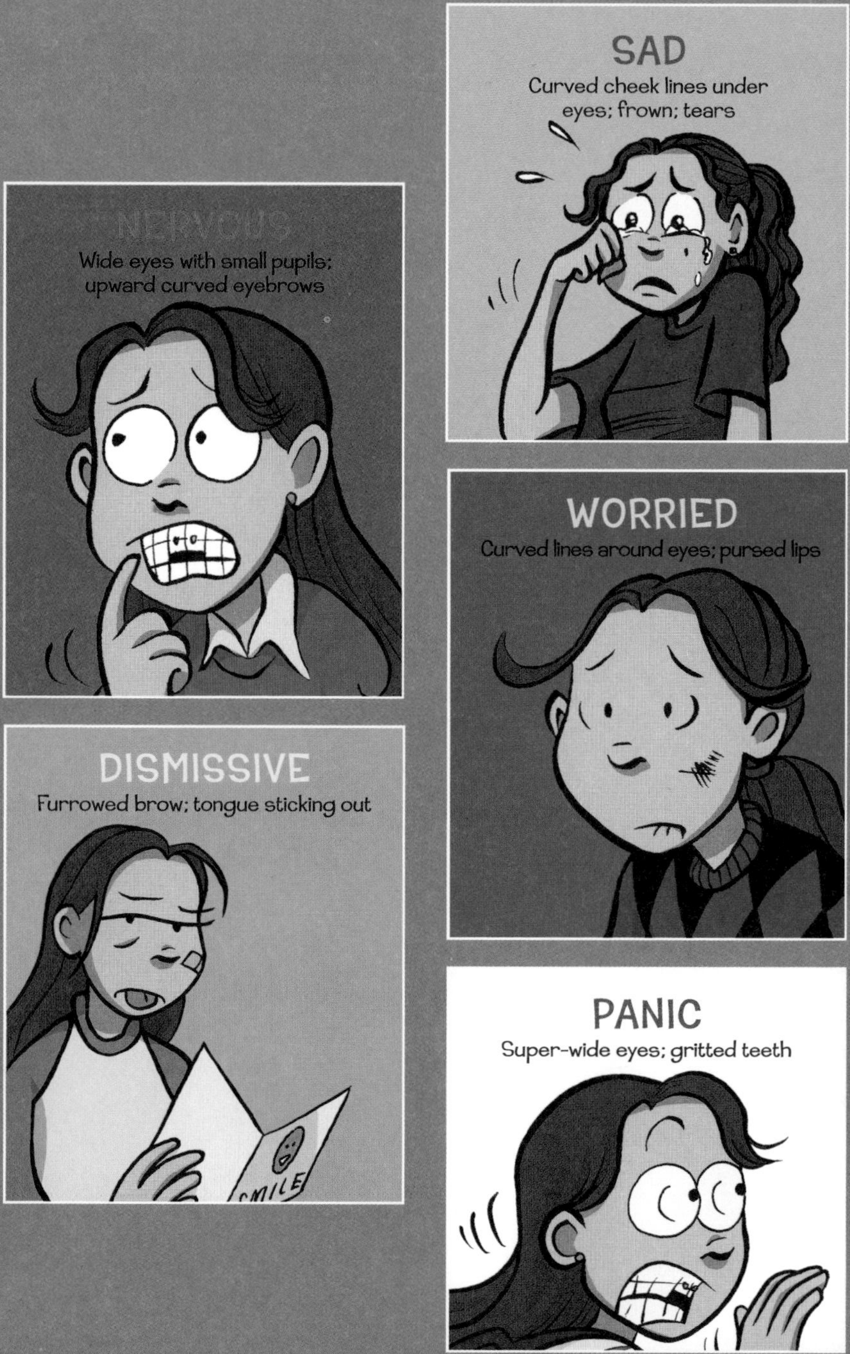
SAD
Curved cheek lines under eyes; frown; tears
NERVOUS
Wide eyes with small pupils; upward curved eyebrows
WORRIED
Curved lines around eyes; pursed lips
DISMISSIVE
Furrowed brow; tongue sticking out
SMILE
PANIC
Super-wide eyes; gritted teeth

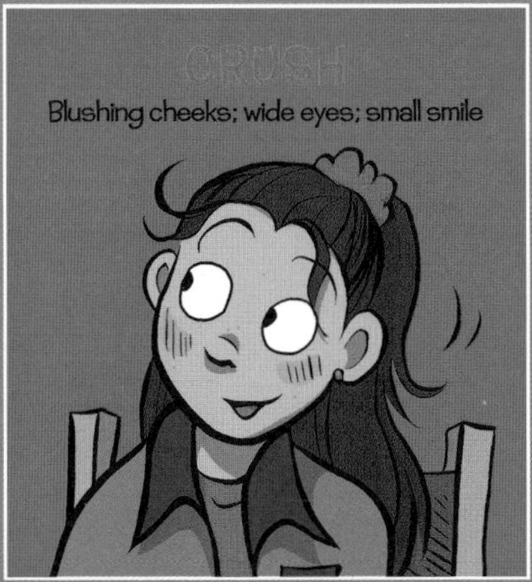
CRUSH
Blushing cheeks; wide eyes; small smile

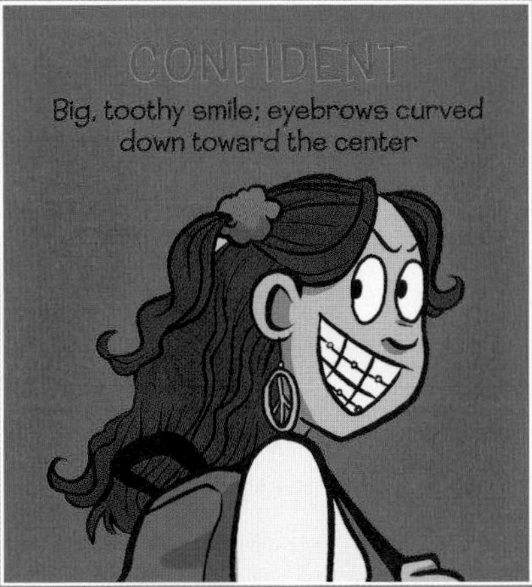
CONFIDENT
Big, toothy smile; eyebrows curved down toward the center

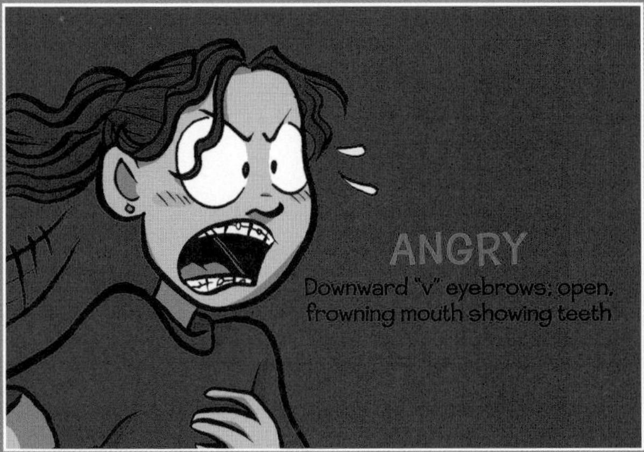
ANGRY
Downward "v" eyebrows; open, frowning mouth showing teeth

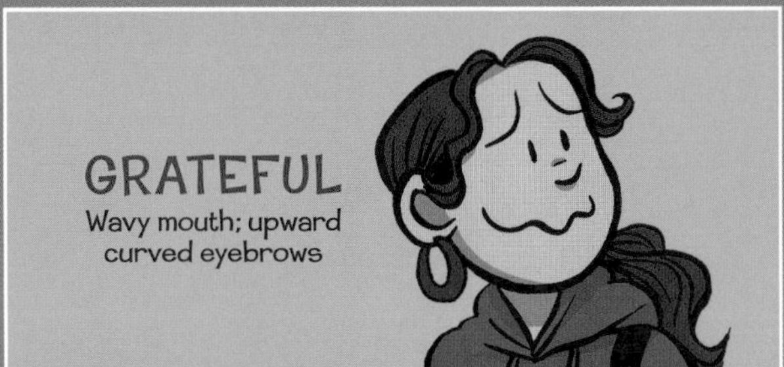
GRATEFUL
Wavy mouth; upward curved eyebrows

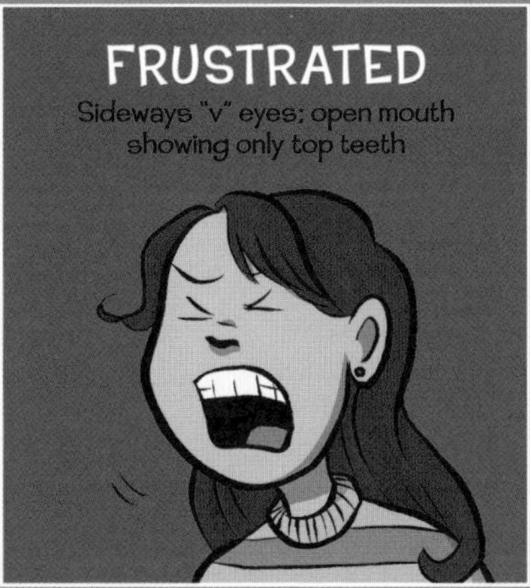
FRUSTRATED
Sideways "v" eyes; open mouth showing only top teeth

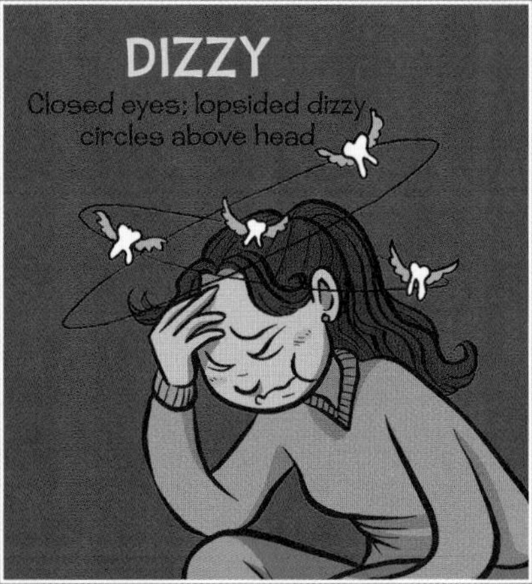
DIZZY
Closed eyes; lopsided dizzy circles above head

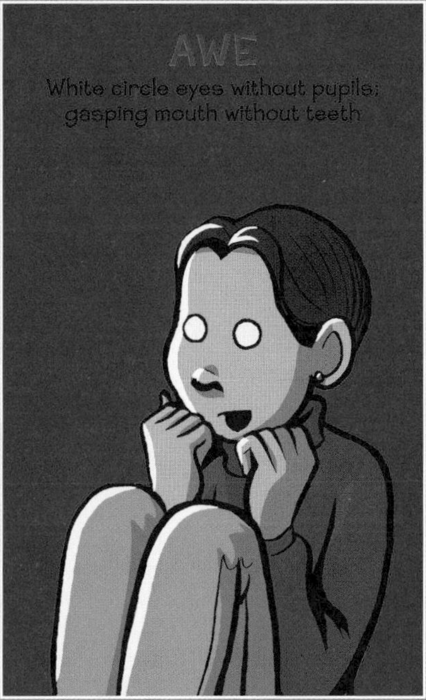
AWE
White circle eyes without pupils; gasping mouth without teeth

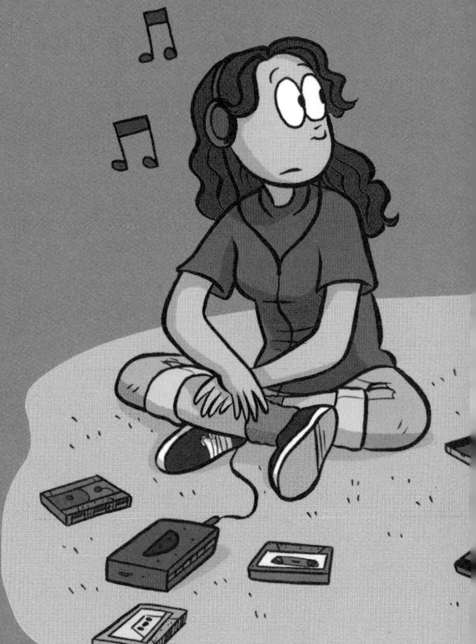

PERSONAL EXPRESSION

Now try drawing your own facial expressions. See how many different moods you can create by changing little details of each facial feature, like eyebrows, eyes, and mouth.

TIP

Try looking in a mirror
to see how your face
changes with your mood.
Then include those
changes in your
drawings!

See how changing one element on the same face can alter the entire expression, like raising or lowering the eyebrows, or changing how wide the eyes are.

TIP

Play with different symbols
around your character's
expressions to help convey
their mood, like question
marks if they're confused,
or hearts if they're
in love.

HOMETOWN INSPIRATION

I grew up in San Francisco, which provided the backdrop for *Smile*. I studied photographs of different places that were important to me when I was younger and added them to my book, including iconic San Francisco landmarks, my family's apartment complex, and my school. Along the way, I wanted to make sure I captured the feelings my hometown evoked. I paid special attention to environmental details like fog, rain, and cityscapes, and even included a major earthquake that my family lived through. The goal is to help readers feel they're experiencing the story in the moment!

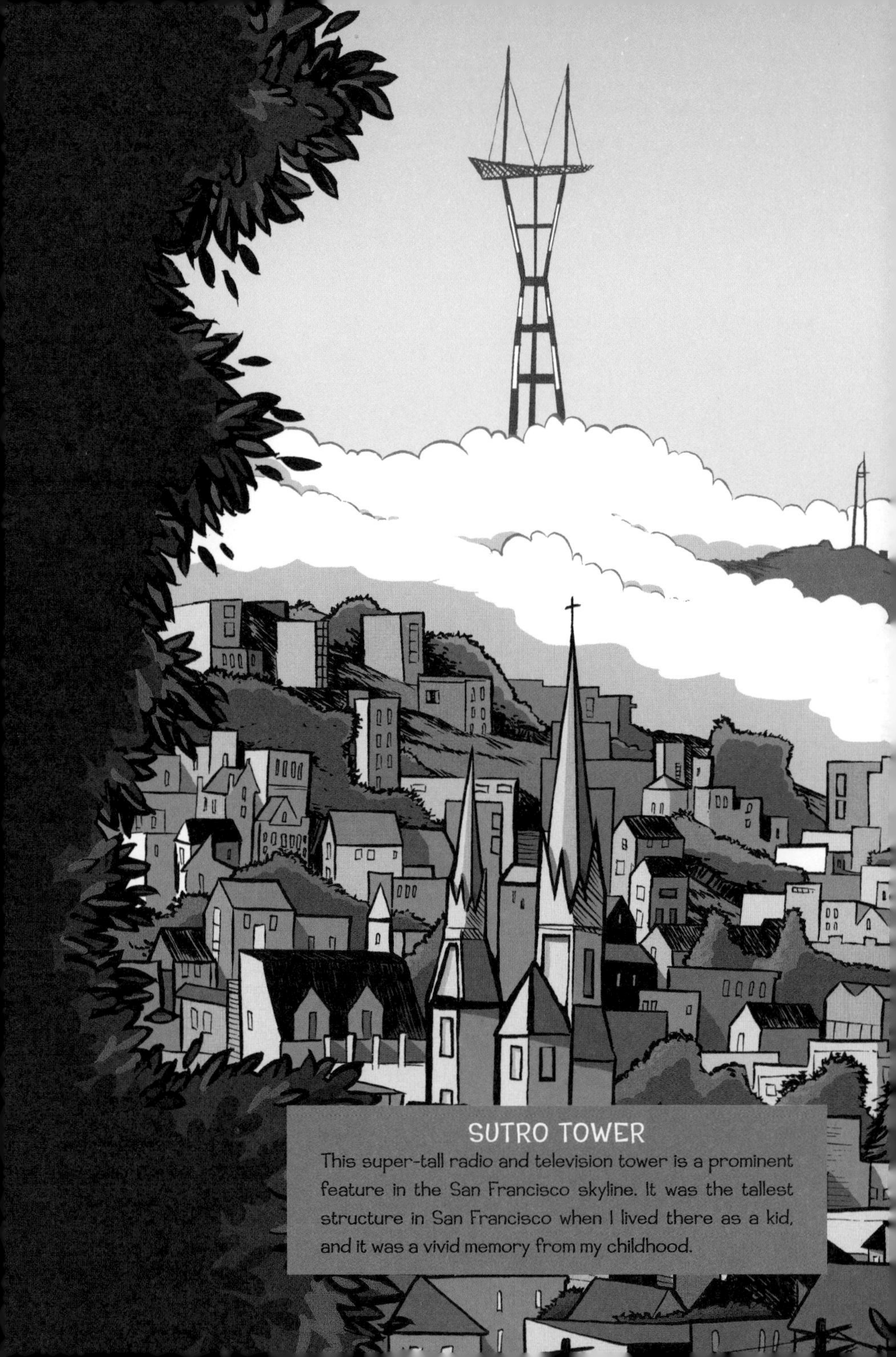

SUTRO TOWER

This super-tall radio and television tower is a prominent feature in the San Francisco skyline. It was the tallest structure in San Francisco when I lived there as a kid, and it was a vivid memory from my childhood.

MY APARTMENT COMPLEX

Growing up in a big city with neighbors all around, I always felt like there was hustle and bustle happening right outside my doorstep.

CITY SKYLINE

But at night, I loved the quiet city skyline that was visible from my window!

MY MIDDLE SCHOOL

San Francisco is filled with lots of different neighborhoods. I wanted to capture their distinct looks, because they are unique to my experience.

MY HIGH SCHOOL

Starting high school was a big deal. Because the school was way bigger than my middle school, it was a chance to meet new people and have new adventures.

EARTHQUAKE

In 1989, San Francisco experienced a major earthquake that caused severe damage throughout the city. Thankfully, my family wasn't affected too badly. But the ordeal made an impression. For a little while, I almost forgot about all the drama going on with my teeth!

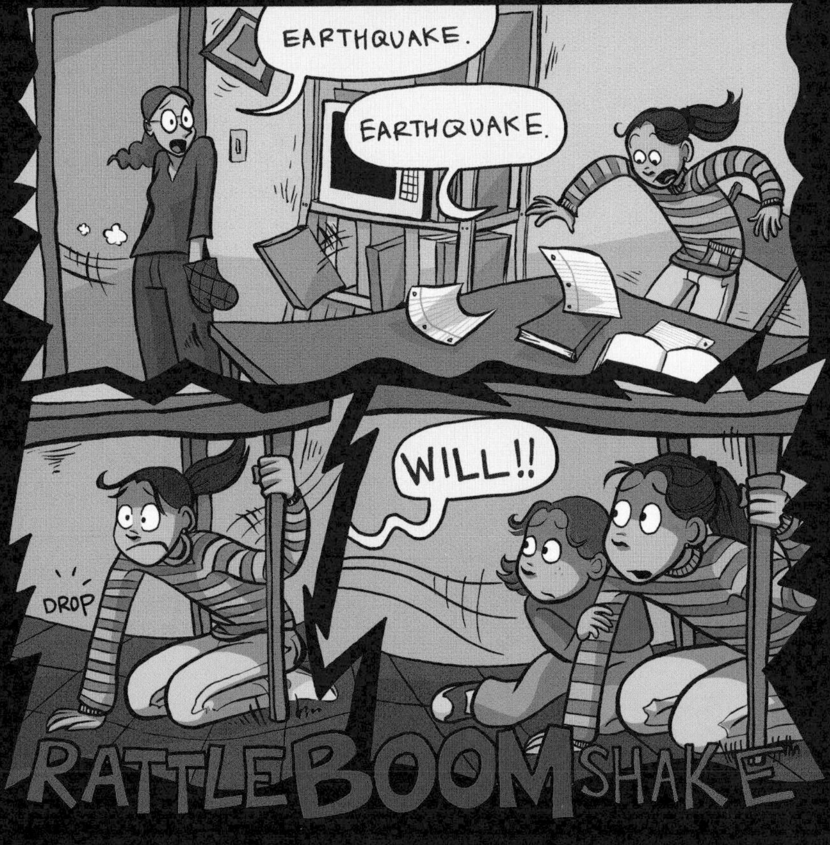
EARTHQUAKE.
EARTHQUAKE.
WILL!!
DROP
RATTLE BOOM SHAKE

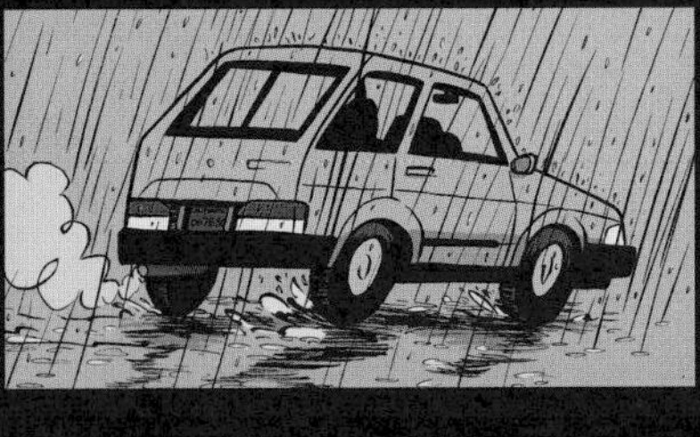

RAIN

The weather in San Francisco can be pretty rainy, foggy, and moody. I wanted to capture that element in my memoir, since it helped reflect my emotions during everything I was going through.

YOUR HOMETOWN

Answer the questions on these pages to reveal how
your hometown has shaped who you are.

Where is your hometown?

What's your favorite thing about your hometown?

Where do you like to hang out?

How would you describe the people in your hometown?

What's the weather usually like?

How does your hometown make you feel?

Describe something in your hometown that
helped shape who you are.

If you could change one thing about your
hometown, what would it be?

What school do you attend?

What's your favorite thing about your school?

What's your least favorite thing about your school?

Describe how you've met different friends.

What makes your hometown and school unique
places to write about?

YOUR HOMETOWN PHOTOS

Use the space below to paste pictures of your hometown. (If you only have digital photos, ask an adult to help you print them.) Don't forget to include captions about what makes each place important to you.

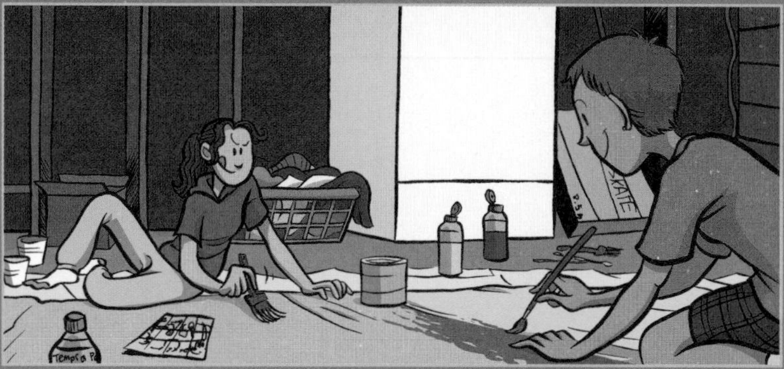
SKATE

SHARING YOUR STORY

It's time to get writing! Use the following pages to write and draw the beginning of your own personal comic narrative. But don't worry if you don't have a great big story idea like my dental drama to write about. It can be as simple as a retelling of a funny family mishap. Or an event that was meaningful to you and helped make you the person you are today. It could even be the tale of an accomplishment that made you really proud. All that matters is that your story is important to you.

STORY IDEAS

Write out three different story ideas that you think would make a cool memoir comic.

WRITE IT!

Choose one of your three ideas and write out the whole story.

STORY TITLE:

_____

_____

_____

_____

_____

_____

_____

_____

_____

_____

_____

_____

_____

_____

_____

_____

_____

_____

_____

_____

_____

_____

_____

_____

_____

_____

_____

_____

_____

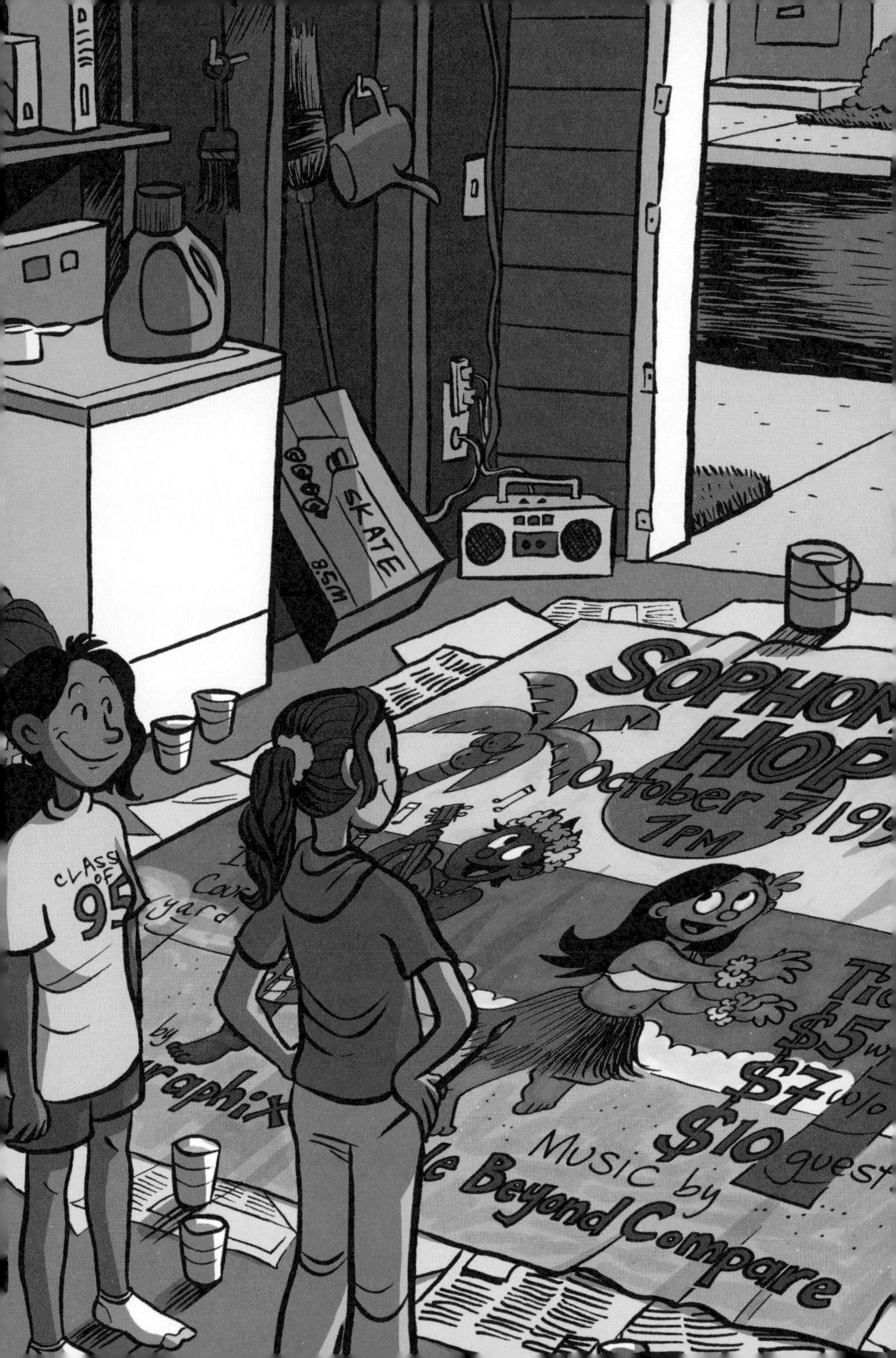
SKATE
8.5M
SOPHOM
HOP
October 7, 199
7PM
CLASS OF 95
Tic
$5 w/
$7 w/o
$10 guest
MUSIC by
le Beyond Compare
by
raphiX

DRAW IT!

Use the panels on these pages to draw the beginning of your story.
Don't forget to include word balloons!

CHAPTER 2
ALL IN THE FAMILY

AN EXCERPT FROM *SISTERS*

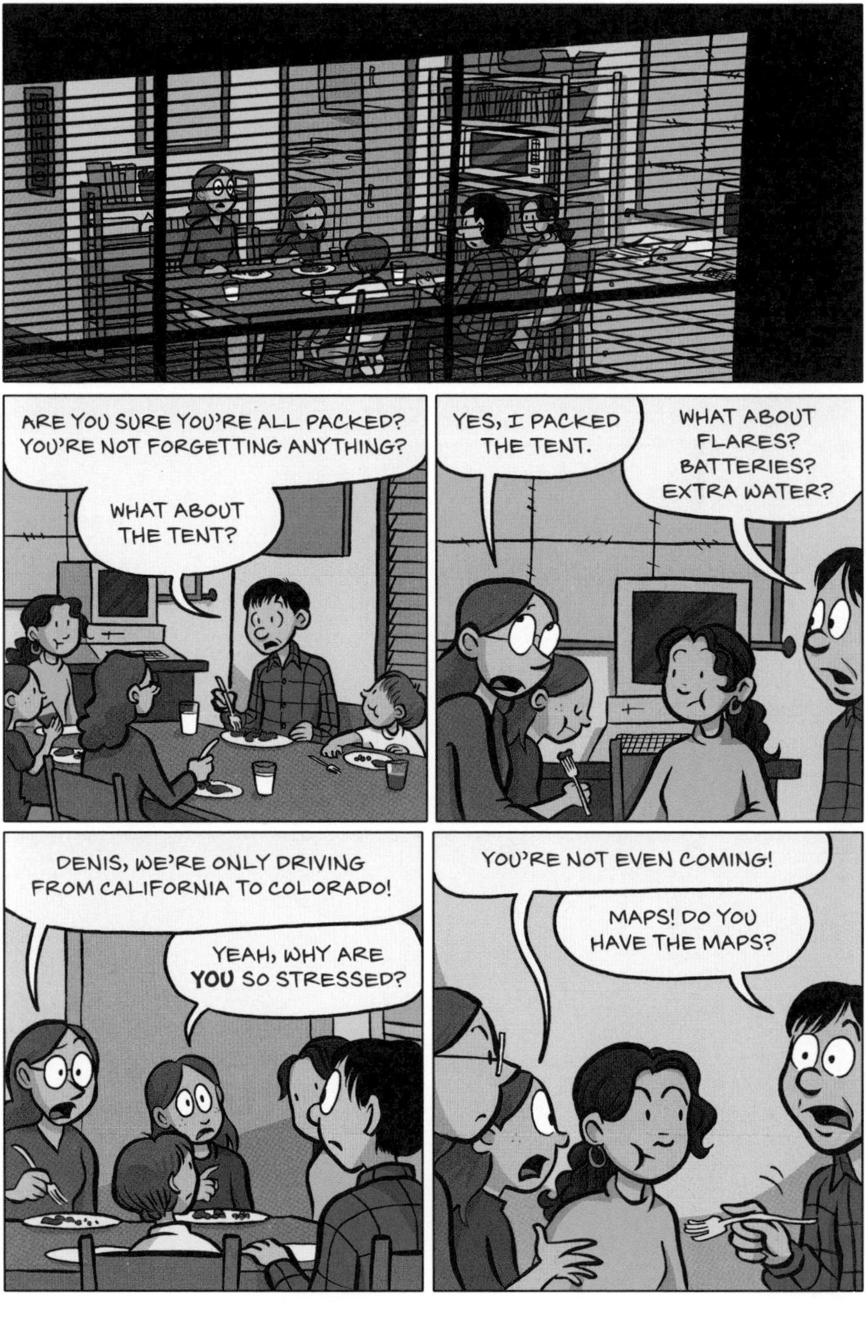
ARE YOU SURE YOU'RE ALL PACKED? YOU'RE NOT FORGETTING ANYTHING?
WHAT ABOUT THE TENT?
YES, I PACKED THE TENT.
WHAT ABOUT FLARES? BATTERIES? EXTRA WATER?
DENIS, WE'RE ONLY DRIVING FROM CALIFORNIA TO COLORADO!
YEAH, WHY ARE **YOU** SO STRESSED?
YOU'RE NOT EVEN COMING!
MAPS! DO YOU HAVE THE MAPS?

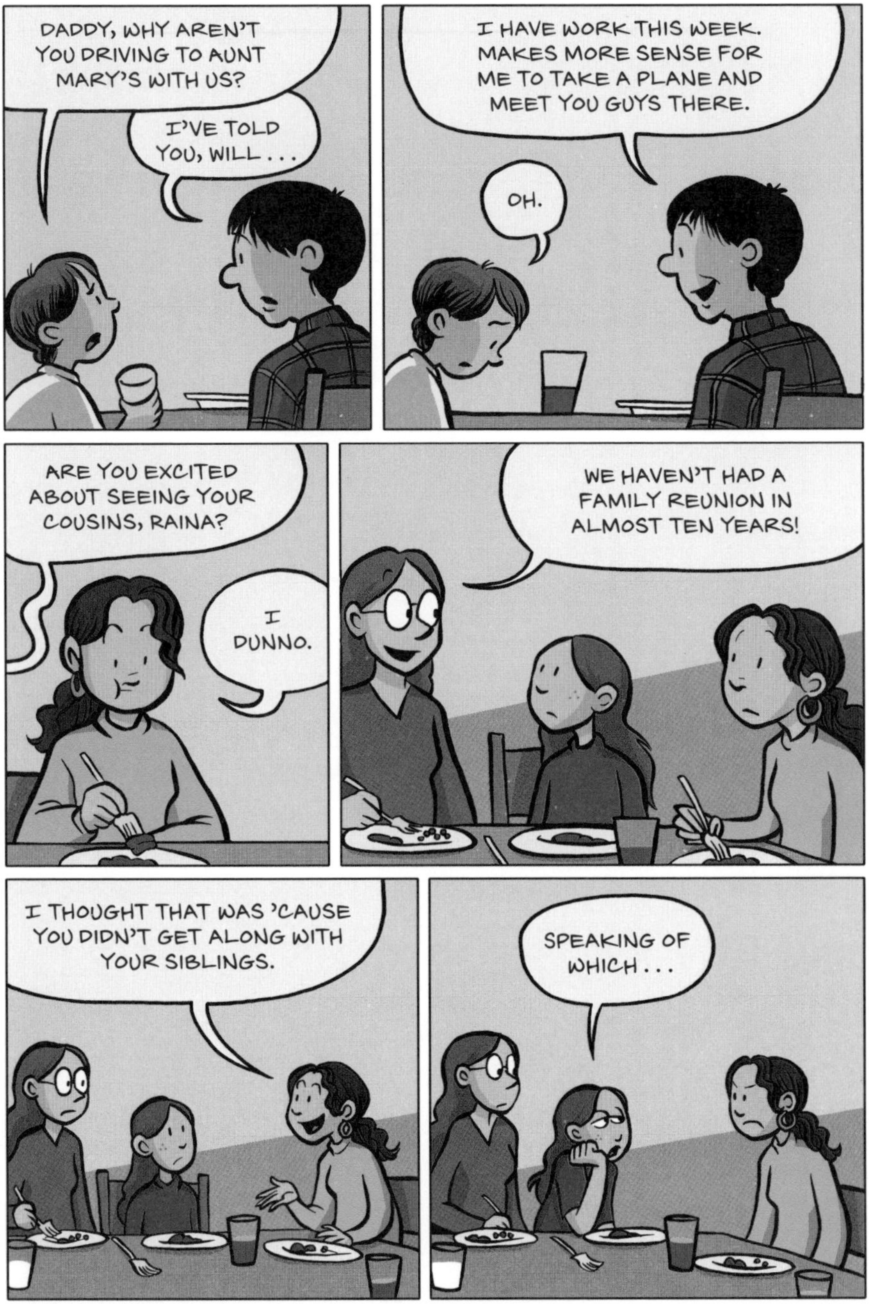
DADDY, WHY AREN'T YOU DRIVING TO AUNT MARY'S WITH US?
I'VE TOLD YOU, WILL . . .
I HAVE WORK THIS WEEK. MAKES MORE SENSE FOR ME TO TAKE A PLANE AND MEET YOU GUYS THERE.
OH.
ARE YOU EXCITED ABOUT SEEING YOUR COUSINS, RAINA?
I DUNNO.
WE HAVEN'T HAD A FAMILY REUNION IN ALMOST TEN YEARS!
I THOUGHT THAT WAS 'CAUSE YOU DIDN'T GET ALONG WITH YOUR SIBLINGS.
SPEAKING OF WHICH . . .

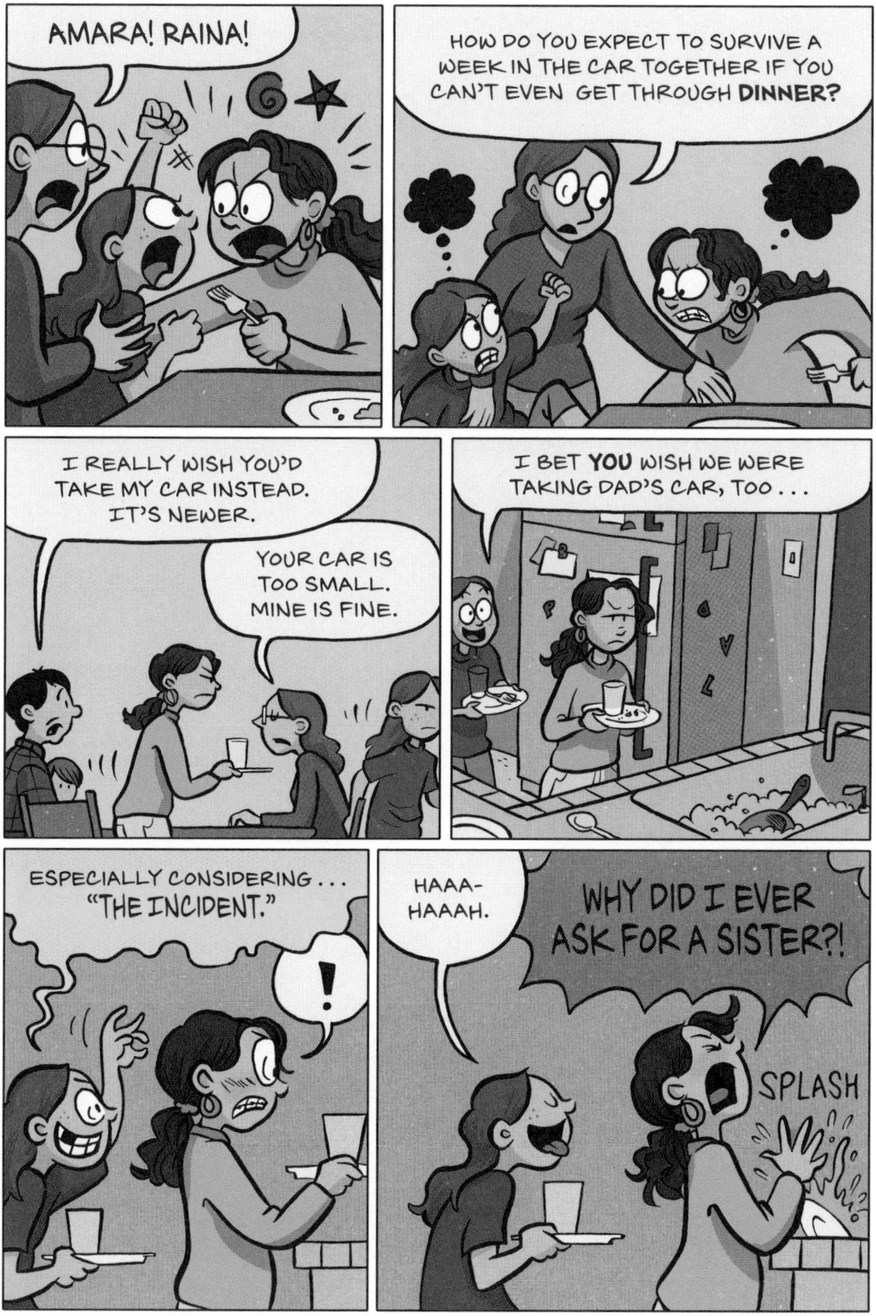
AMARA! RAINA!
HOW DO YOU EXPECT TO SURVIVE A WEEK IN THE CAR TOGETHER IF YOU CAN'T EVEN GET THROUGH **DINNER?**
I REALLY WISH YOU'D TAKE MY CAR INSTEAD. IT'S NEWER.
YOUR CAR IS TOO SMALL. MINE IS FINE.
I BET **YOU** WISH WE WERE TAKING DAD'S CAR, TOO . . .
ESPECIALLY CONSIDERING . . . "THE INCIDENT."
!
HAAA-HAAAH.
WHY DID I EVER ASK FOR A SISTER?!
SPLASH

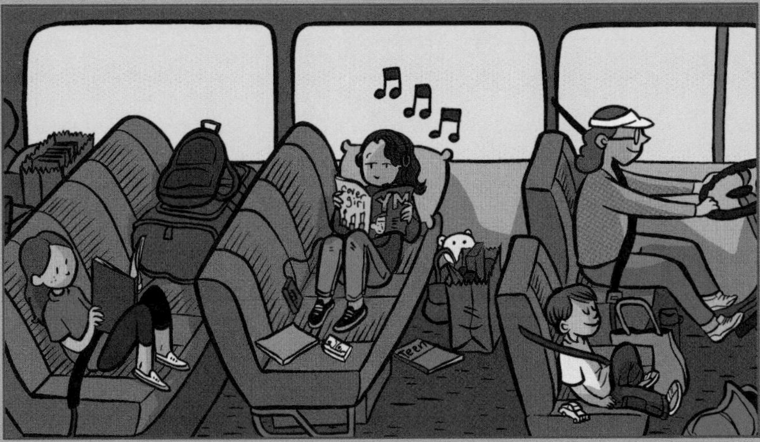
YM

FAMILY INSPIRATION

When I was four years old, I told my parents that I wanted a sister. I thought having a sister would mean having an instant playmate! We'd laugh together, draw together, play games and dress up dolls together, and most importantly, be best friends.

Then my little sister was born, and it wasn't quite what I expected. First of all, she was a baby (cute, but not really able to play dolls). Then later, she was a toddler (and wanted to take my dolls). As we grew older, we eventually did learn to play together. But we also learned to argue, antagonize, mutually coexist, and love each other as only sisters can.

My graphic novel *Sisters* was inspired by a weeklong road trip I took with my mom, sister, and younger brother the summer before I started high school. That trip was a turning point for my sister and me. We still got on each other's nerves, but we also bonded in a way that would change our lives forever.

Family is a huge part of who I am. The funny memories that glue us together work their way into my storytelling every day.

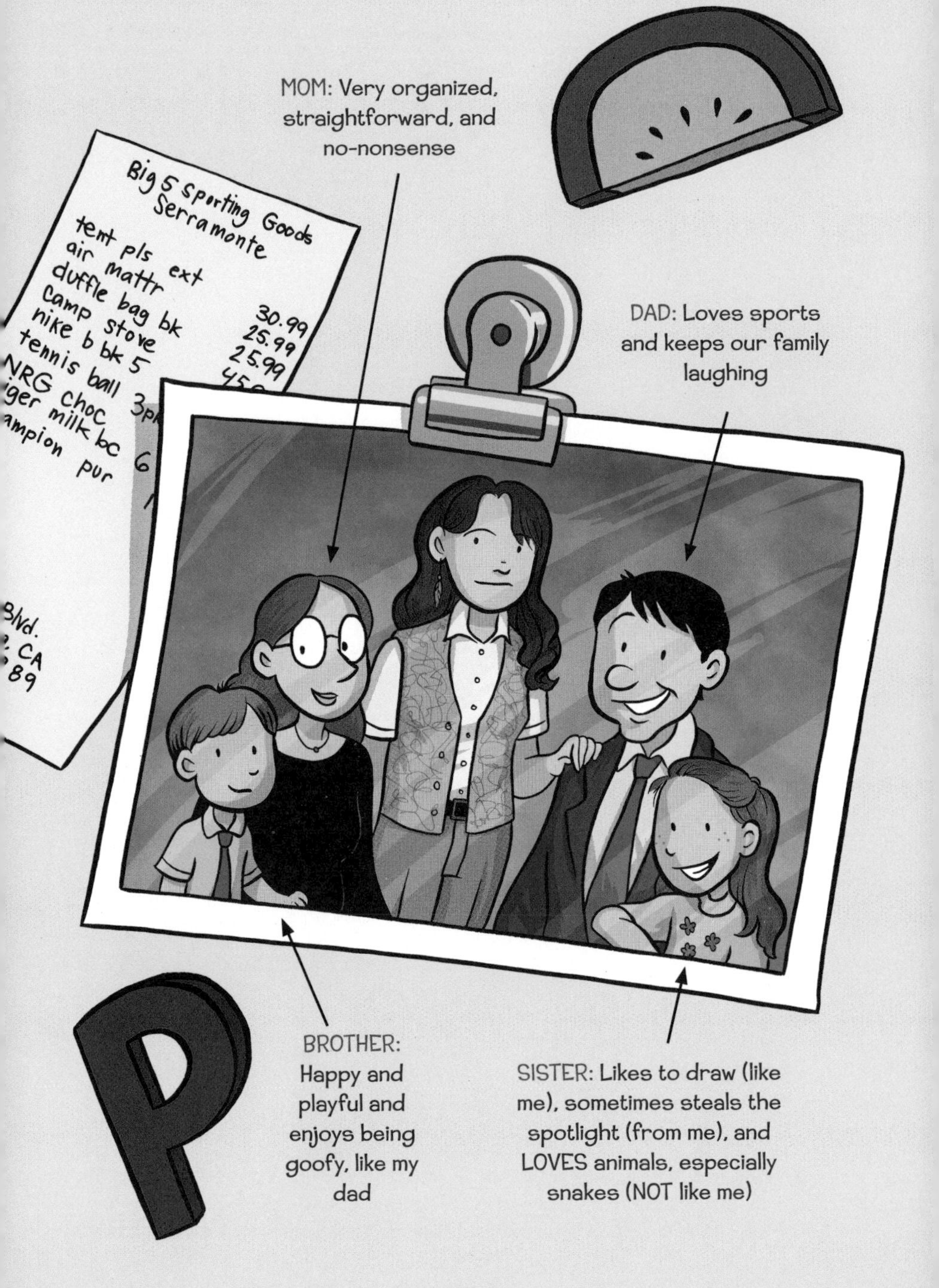
MOM: Very organized, straightforward, and no-nonsense
Big 5 Sporting Goods
Serramonte
tent pls ext
air mattr
duffle bag bk 30.99
camp stove 25.99
nike b bk 5 25.99
tennis ball
NRG choc
DAD: Loves sports and keeps our family laughing
BROTHER: Happy and playful and enjoys being goofy, like my dad
SISTER: Likes to draw (like me), sometimes steals the spotlight (from me), and LOVES animals, especially snakes (NOT like me)

SISTER SNAPSHOTS

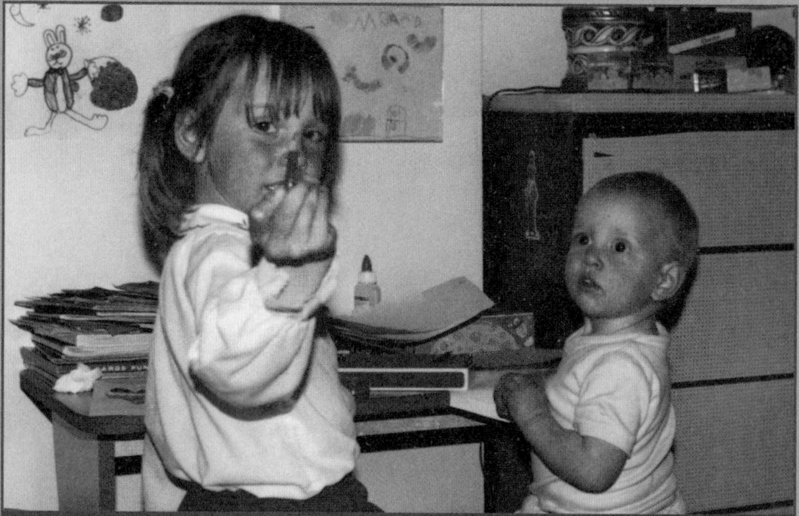

After I wrote the script for *Sisters*, my dad sent me this photo, which I had forgotten about. This picture pretty much encapsulates that story in a nutshell. We're about six and one here.

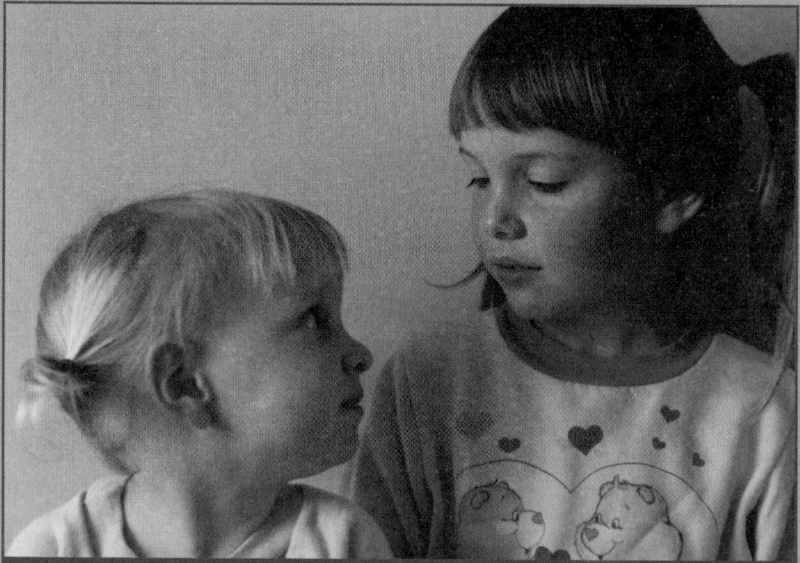

My mom took this picture of Amara and me sitting on top of a hamper in our upstairs hallway. The photo still hangs in the same spot.

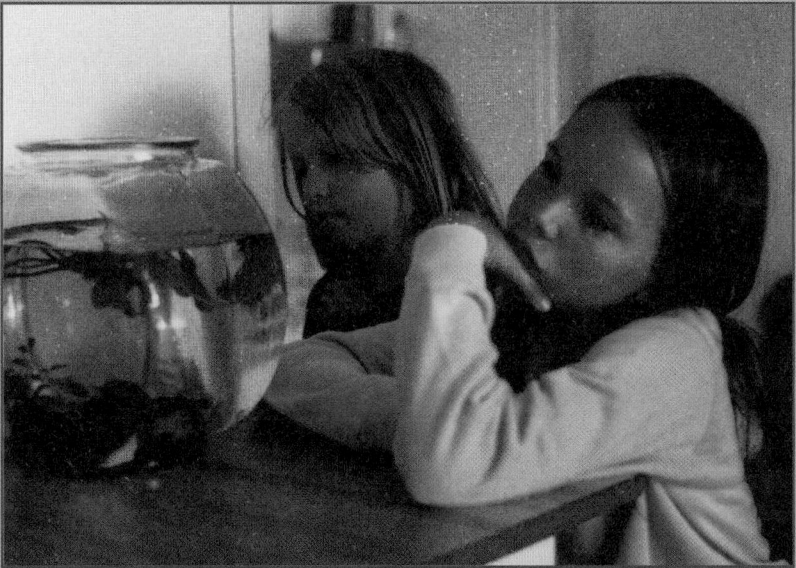

Goldfish. We look pretty excited, don't we?

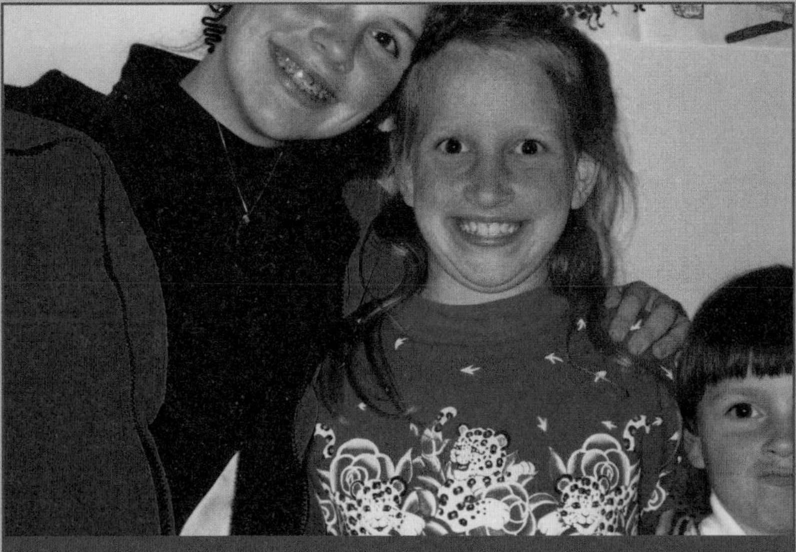

Here we are around the time *Sisters* takes place: ages fourteen, nine, and six. Amara had just won first place in an art contest I'd gotten an honorable mention for, a few years prior. I'm hiding my jealousy well!

YOUR FAMILY

What makes your family an integral part of your story?
Write down your answers to these questions to find out!

Who is in your family?

How would you describe each of your family members?

What do you love most about your family?

What are some things that drive you nuts about your family?

What are your silliest family memories?

Do you have a family tradition? Describe it!

What's something that's super unique to your family?

Do you have any distant relatives? Who are they?
How often do you see them?

What's one important thing your family has taught you?

How does your family show you they love you?

How do you show your family you love them?

What's the toughest situation you and
your family have ever had to face?

How did you get through it together?

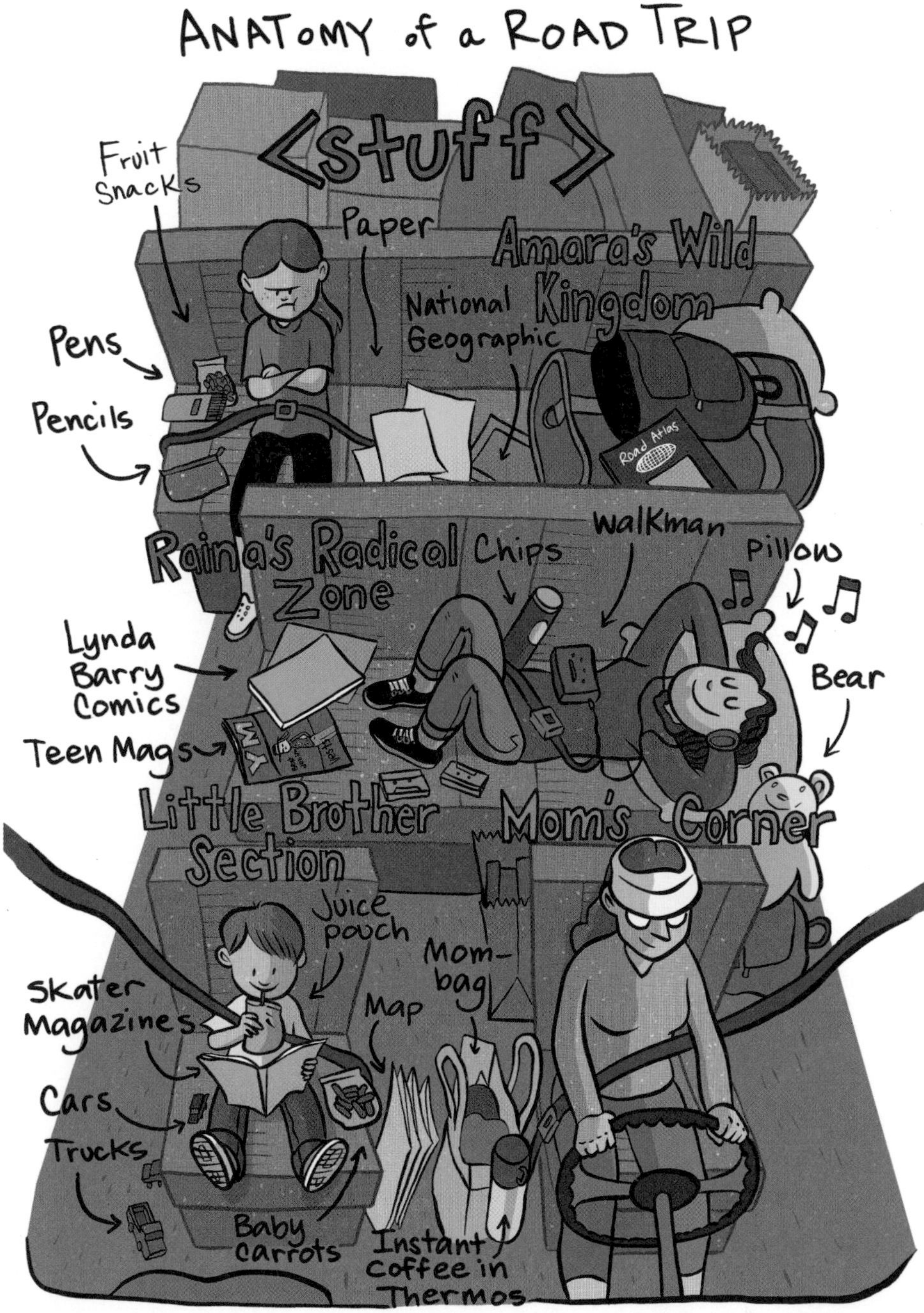
ANATOMY of a ROAD TRIP
<stuff>
Fruit Snacks
Paper
Amara's Wild Kingdom
National Geographic
Pens
Pencils
Road Atlas
Raina's Radical Zone
Chips
Walkman
Pillow
Lynda Barry Comics
Bear
Teen Mags
YM
Little Brother Section
Mom's Corner
Juice pouch
Mom-bag
Skater Magazines
Map
Cars
Trucks
Baby carrots
Instant coffee in Thermos

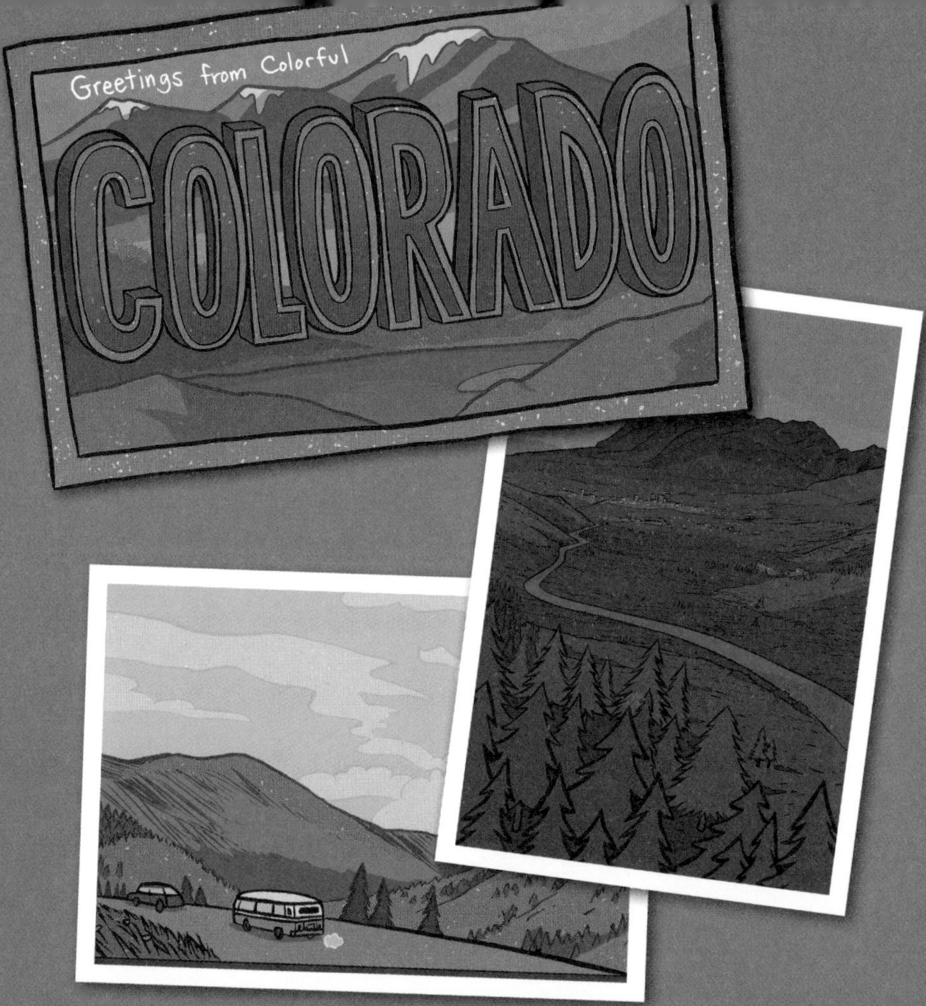
Greetings from Colorful
COLORADO

HITTING THE ROAD

New places and new adventures can inspire you in unexpected ways. Growing up in San Francisco, I was accustomed to life in a big city: lots of people, noise, and built-up cityscapes. Taking a family road trip from California to Colorado meant that I was stuck in a van with my siblings for a whole week, but it also meant that we got to see breathtaking views from unique vantage points together. Deserts. Mountains. Vast starry skies. It was the first time I'd ever seen so much natural beauty, and I loved being able to share it with my family.

YOUR TRAVEL MEMORIES

Think of any kind of trip you've been on, whether it's been to forests, beaches, foreign cities, or a family member's house, and use these questions to share how different travel adventures inspire you!

What is your favorite place you've ever traveled?

If you could go anywhere in the world, where would it be? Why?

How does going to new places make you feel?

How do you get ready for a family vacation?

What's your favorite family travel memory?

Have you ever had a funny (or not so funny) travel mishap? Share it!

What's your favorite way to travel? On foot? Car? Train? Plane?

What destinations inspire you? How?

What one travel tip would you share with your best friend?

if you could bring only three things with you on a weeklong
road trip, what would they be and why?

Who are your favorite people to travel with?
What makes them so much fun?

Describe a time when taking a special trip
changed your outlook on things:

TELL YOUR FAMILY TRAVEL STORY

Now that you've got the hang of it from the *Smile* section, it's time to share your family travel story! Like before, don't worry if it's not an epic saga (or, in my case, road trip). Your story could be about any special travel experience you've shared with people you love. Just make sure to include how the trip made you feel and what was meaningful about experiencing it with others.

STORY IDEAS

Write out three different story ideas that you think would make a great travel tale.

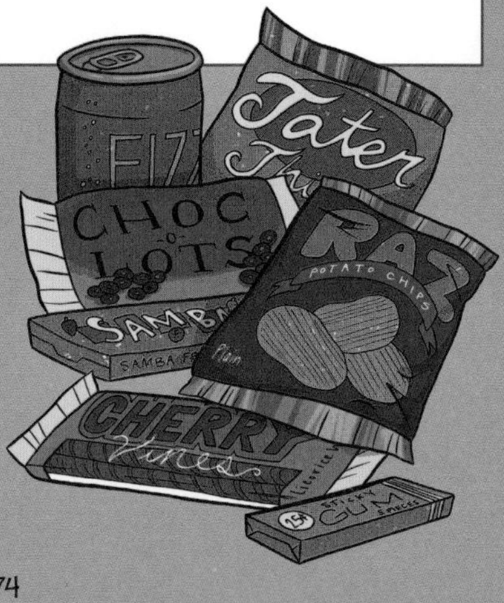

FIZZ
Tater
CHOC-O-LOTS
RAZ
POTATO CHIPS
Plain
SAMBA
CHERRY
STICKY GUM

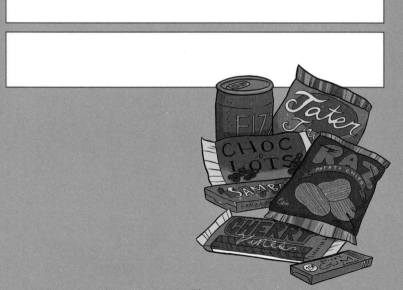

WRITE IT!

Choose one of your three ideas and write out the whole story.

STORY TITLE:

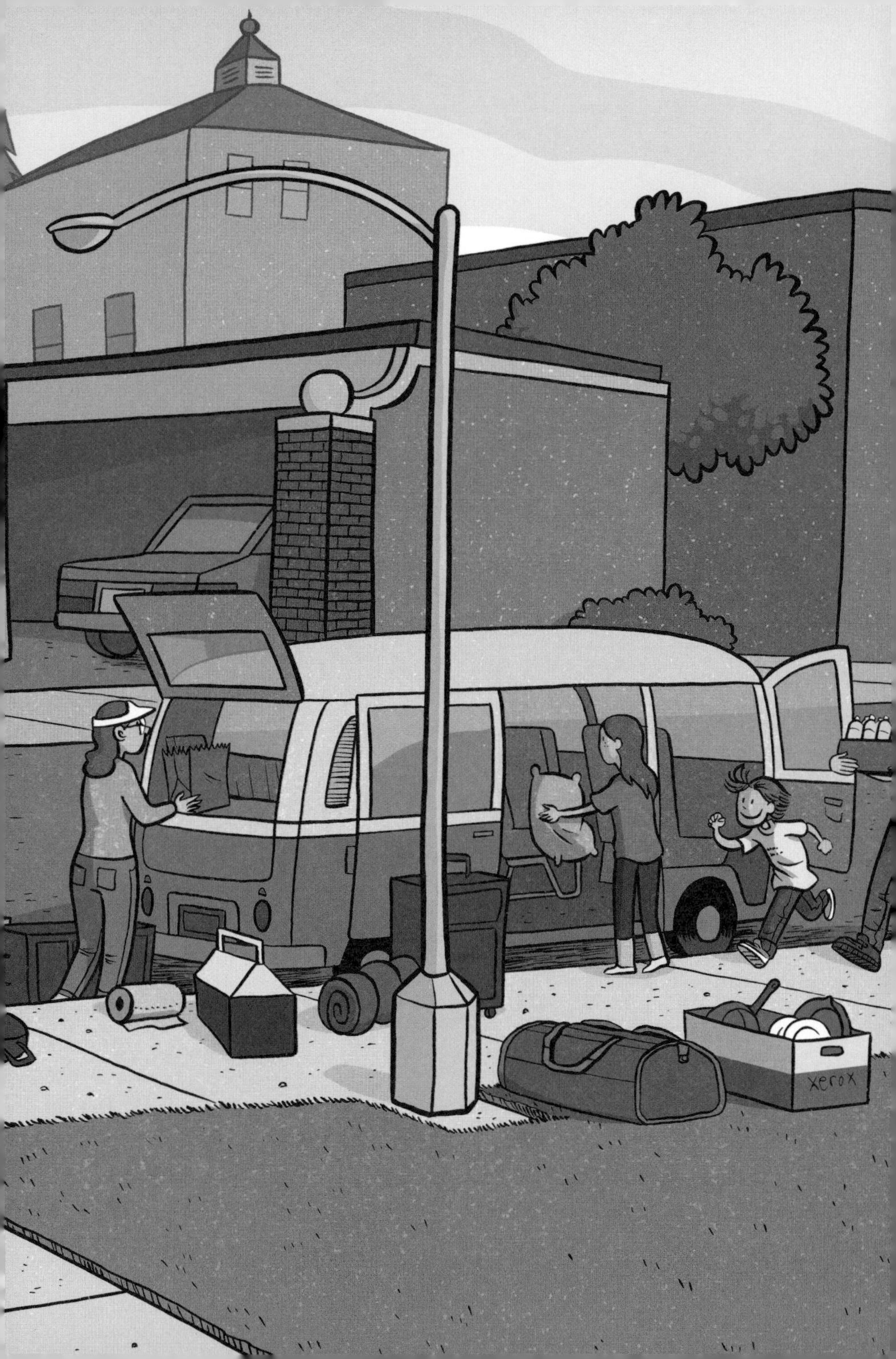
xerox

DRAW IT!

Use the panels on these pages to draw the beginning of your story.
Don't forget to include word balloons!

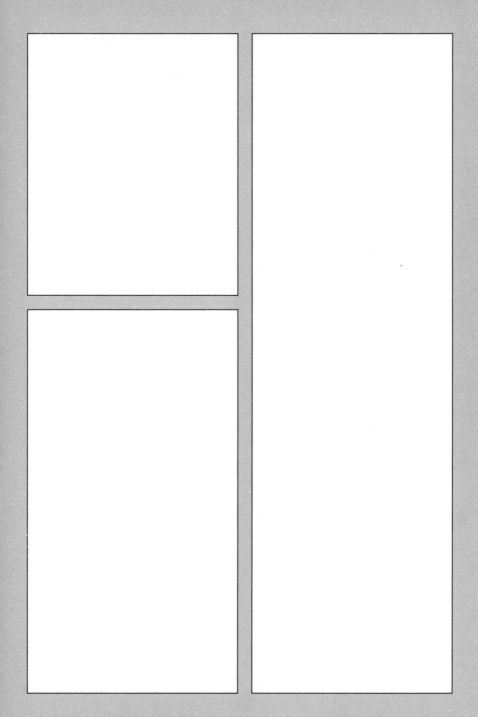

CHAPTER 3
THE DRAMA OF SCHOOL

AN EXCERPT FROM *DRAMA*

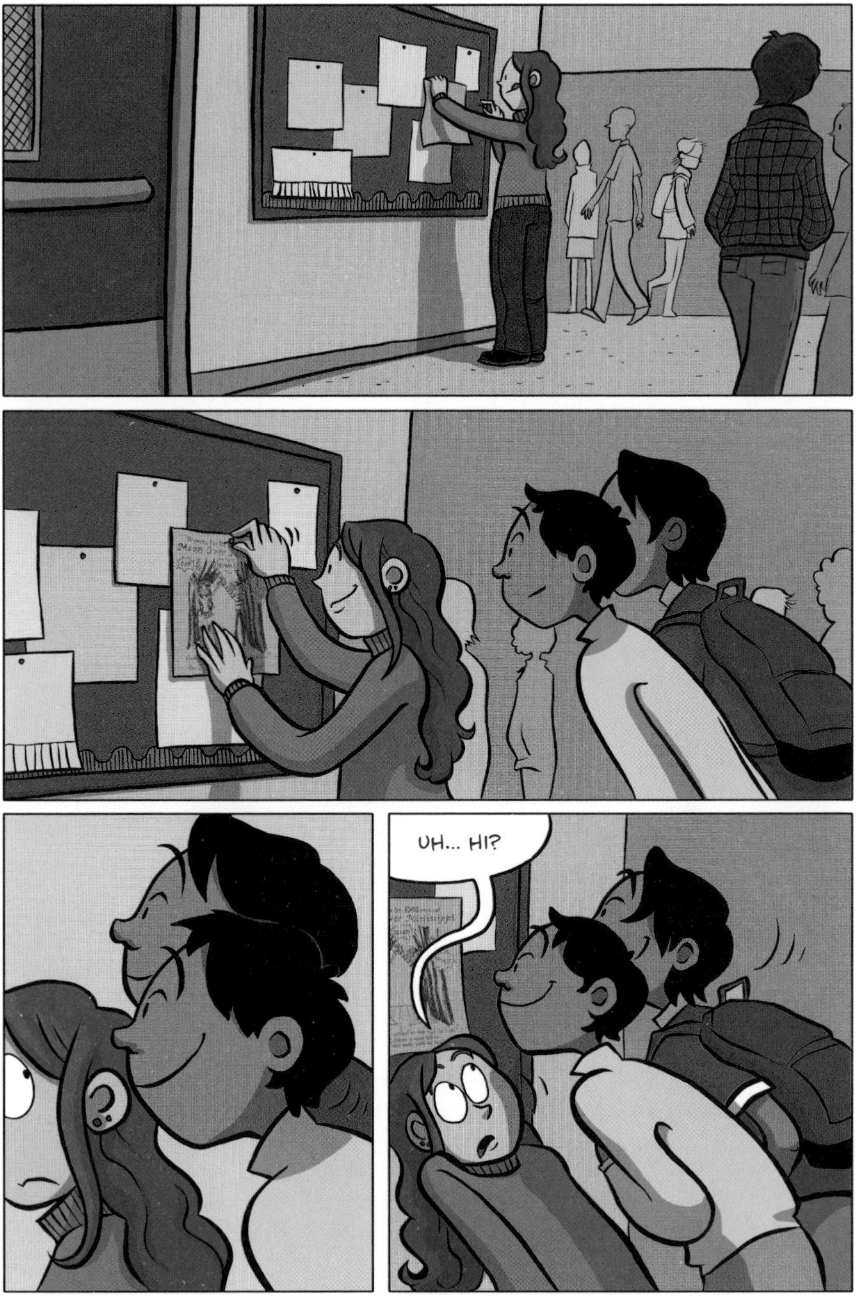
UH... HI?

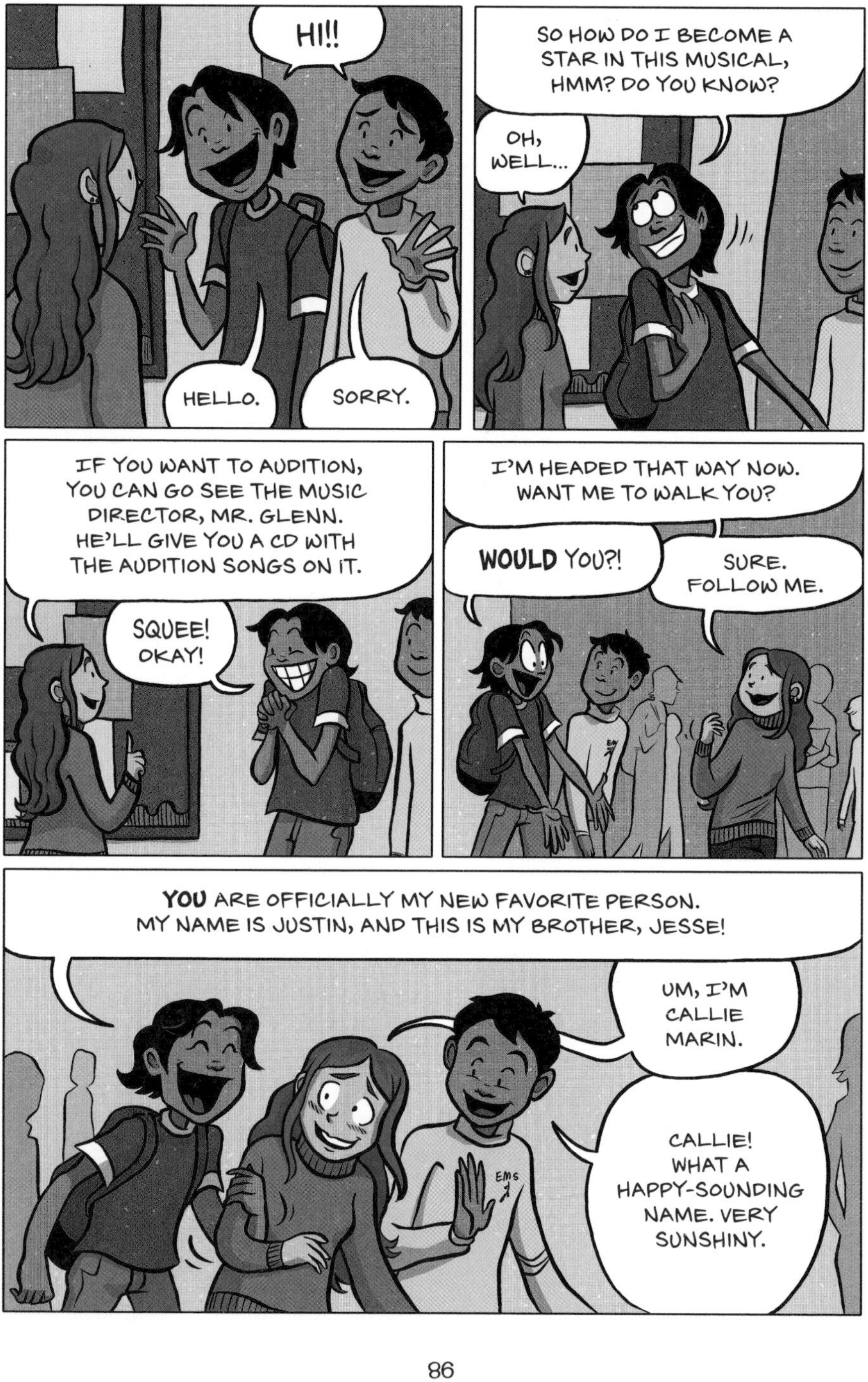
HI!!
HELLO.
SORRY.
SO HOW DO I BECOME A STAR IN THIS MUSICAL, HMM? DO YOU KNOW?
OH, WELL...
IF YOU WANT TO AUDITION, YOU CAN GO SEE THE MUSIC DIRECTOR, MR. GLENN. HE'LL GIVE YOU A CD WITH THE AUDITION SONGS ON IT.
SQUEE! OKAY!
I'M HEADED THAT WAY NOW. WANT ME TO WALK YOU?
WOULD YOU?!
SURE. FOLLOW ME.
YOU ARE OFFICIALLY MY NEW FAVORITE PERSON. MY NAME IS JUSTIN, AND THIS IS MY BROTHER, JESSE!
UM, I'M CALLIE MARIN.
CALLIE! WHAT A HAPPY-SOUNDING NAME. VERY SUNSHINY.

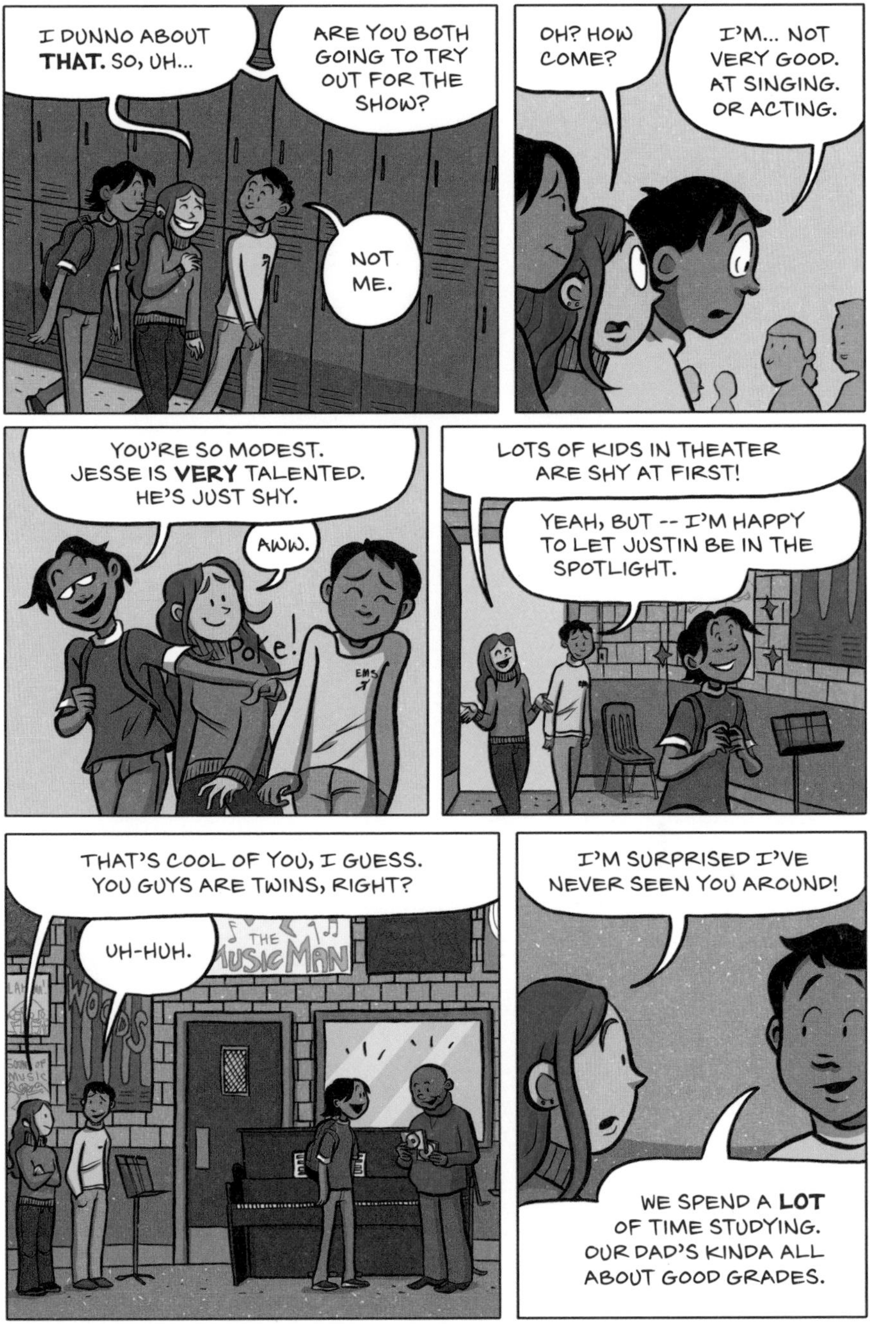
I DUNNO ABOUT **THAT.** SO, UH...
ARE YOU BOTH GOING TO TRY OUT FOR THE SHOW?
NOT ME.
OH? HOW COME?
I'M... NOT VERY GOOD. AT SINGING. OR ACTING.
YOU'RE SO MODEST. JESSE IS **VERY** TALENTED. HE'S JUST SHY.
AWW.
POKE!
EMS
LOTS OF KIDS IN THEATER ARE SHY AT FIRST!
YEAH, BUT -- I'M HAPPY TO LET JUSTIN BE IN THE SPOTLIGHT.
THAT'S COOL OF YOU, I GUESS. YOU GUYS ARE TWINS, RIGHT?
UH-HUH.
THE MUSIC MAN
I'M SURPRISED I'VE NEVER SEEN YOU AROUND!
WE SPEND A **LOT** OF TIME STUDYING. OUR DAD'S KINDA ALL ABOUT GOOD GRADES.

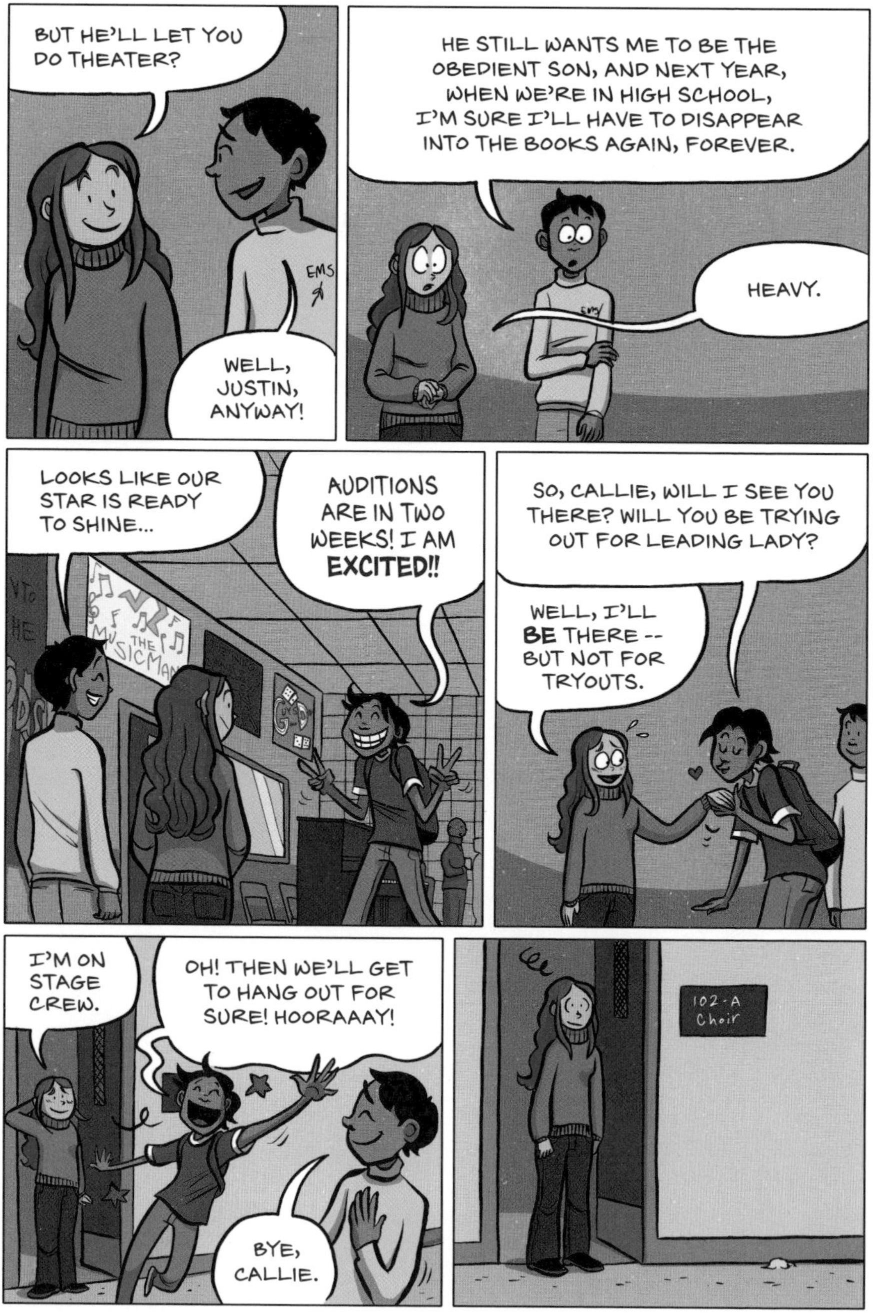
BUT HE'LL LET YOU DO THEATER?
WELL, JUSTIN, ANYWAY!
EMS
HE STILL WANTS ME TO BE THE OBEDIENT SON, AND NEXT YEAR, WHEN WE'RE IN HIGH SCHOOL, I'M SURE I'LL HAVE TO DISAPPEAR INTO THE BOOKS AGAIN, FOREVER.
HEAVY.
LOOKS LIKE OUR STAR IS READY TO SHINE...
AUDITIONS ARE IN TWO WEEKS! I AM **EXCITED!!**
THE MUSIC MAN
SO, CALLIE, WILL I SEE YOU THERE? WILL YOU BE TRYING OUT FOR LEADING LADY?
WELL, I'LL **BE** THERE -- BUT NOT FOR TRYOUTS.
I'M ON STAGE CREW.
OH! THEN WE'LL GET TO HANG OUT FOR SURE! HOORAAAY!
BYE, CALLIE.
102-A Choir

CLASS ACT

Drama is a fictional graphic novel that's inspired by my theater-club activities in middle school and high school. Even though the characters are mostly from my imagination, the experiences they encounter (and yes, the drama that ensues) are very much influenced by real-life events. The one-of-a-kind highs and lows of going to school are a perfect source for story ideas. Whether you're into sports, art, music, are focused on hitting the books, or all of the above, I'm sure you'll agree that drama club isn't the only place with drama going on!

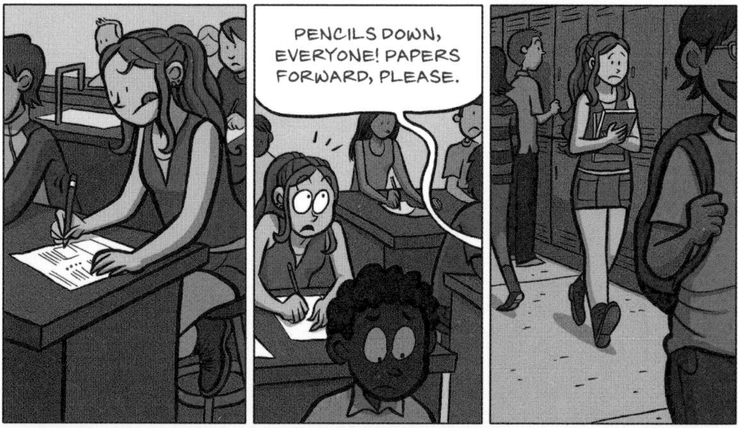
PENCILS DOWN, EVERYONE! PAPERS FORWARD, PLEASE.

Drama in the classroom

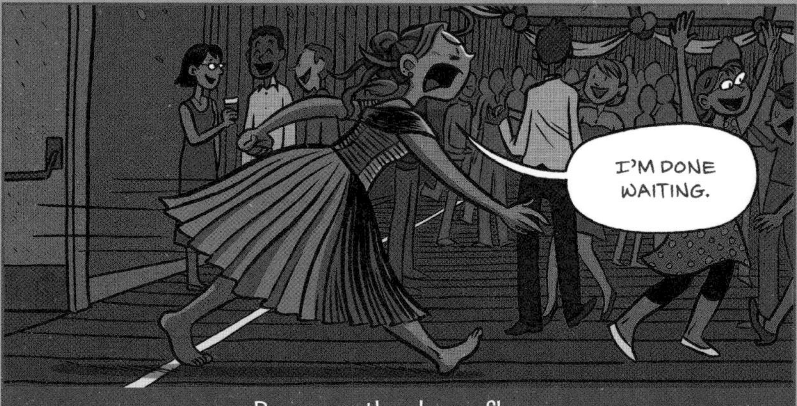
I'M DONE WAITING.

Drama on the dance floor

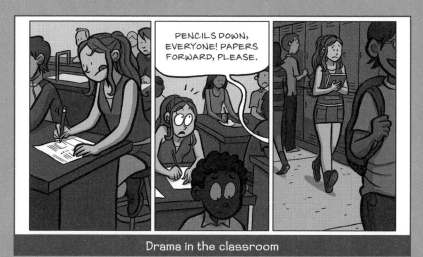

SCHOOL STORIES

What crazy, exciting, nerve-racking, or triumphant events
have shaped your academic experience? Answer these
questions to help get your school story started!

What's your favorite class in school?

What's your least favorite?

What's the craziest thing you've ever seen happen in class?

Who's your favorite teacher? What makes them the best?

Which school subjects are you really good at?

Was there a time you had to work extra hard to
succeed in a class? How did you do it?

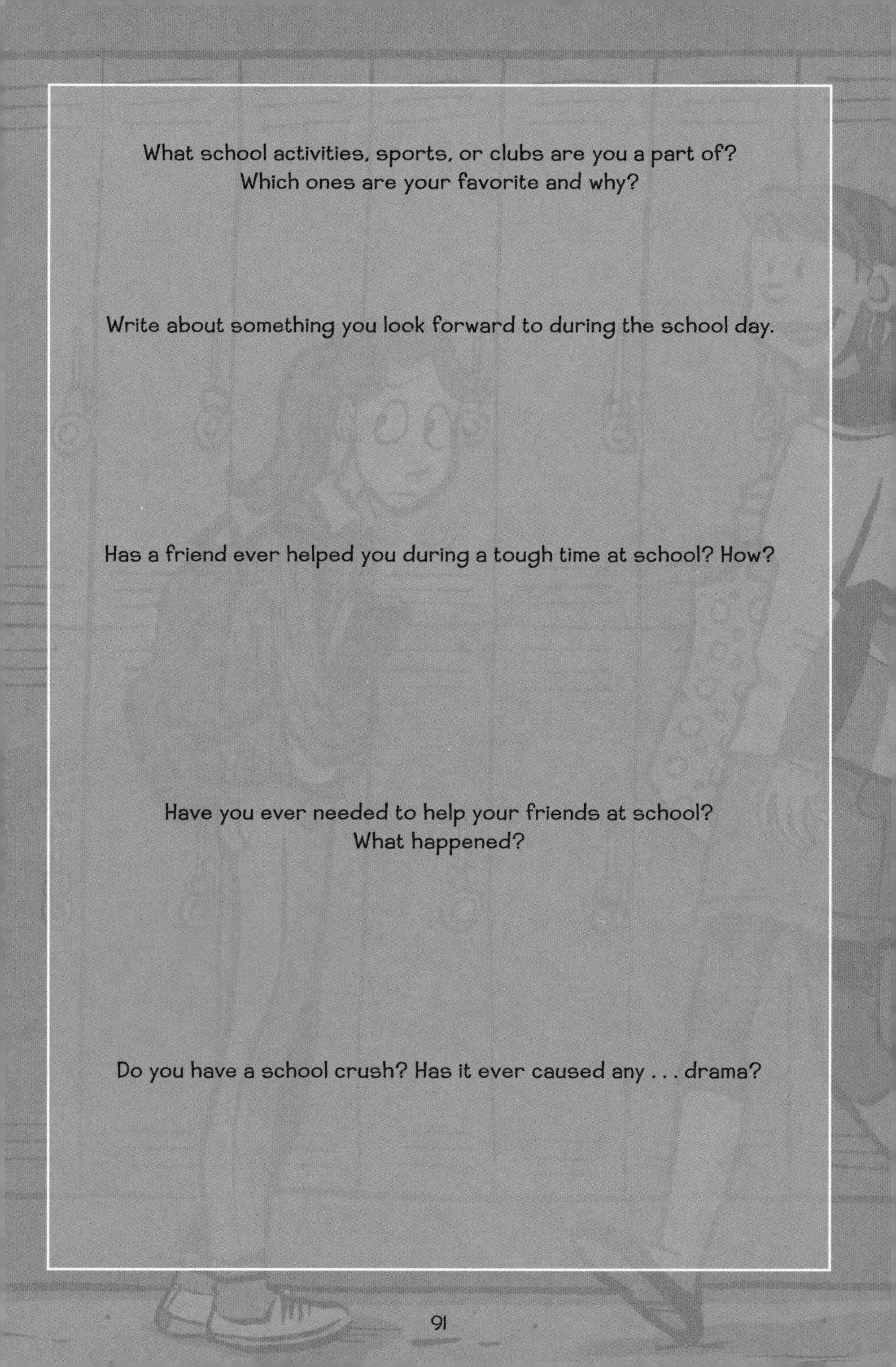

What school activities, sports, or clubs are you a part of?
Which ones are your favorite and why?

Write about something you look forward to during the school day.

Has a friend ever helped you during a tough time at school? How?

Have you ever needed to help your friends at school?
What happened?

Do you have a school crush? Has it ever caused any . . . drama?

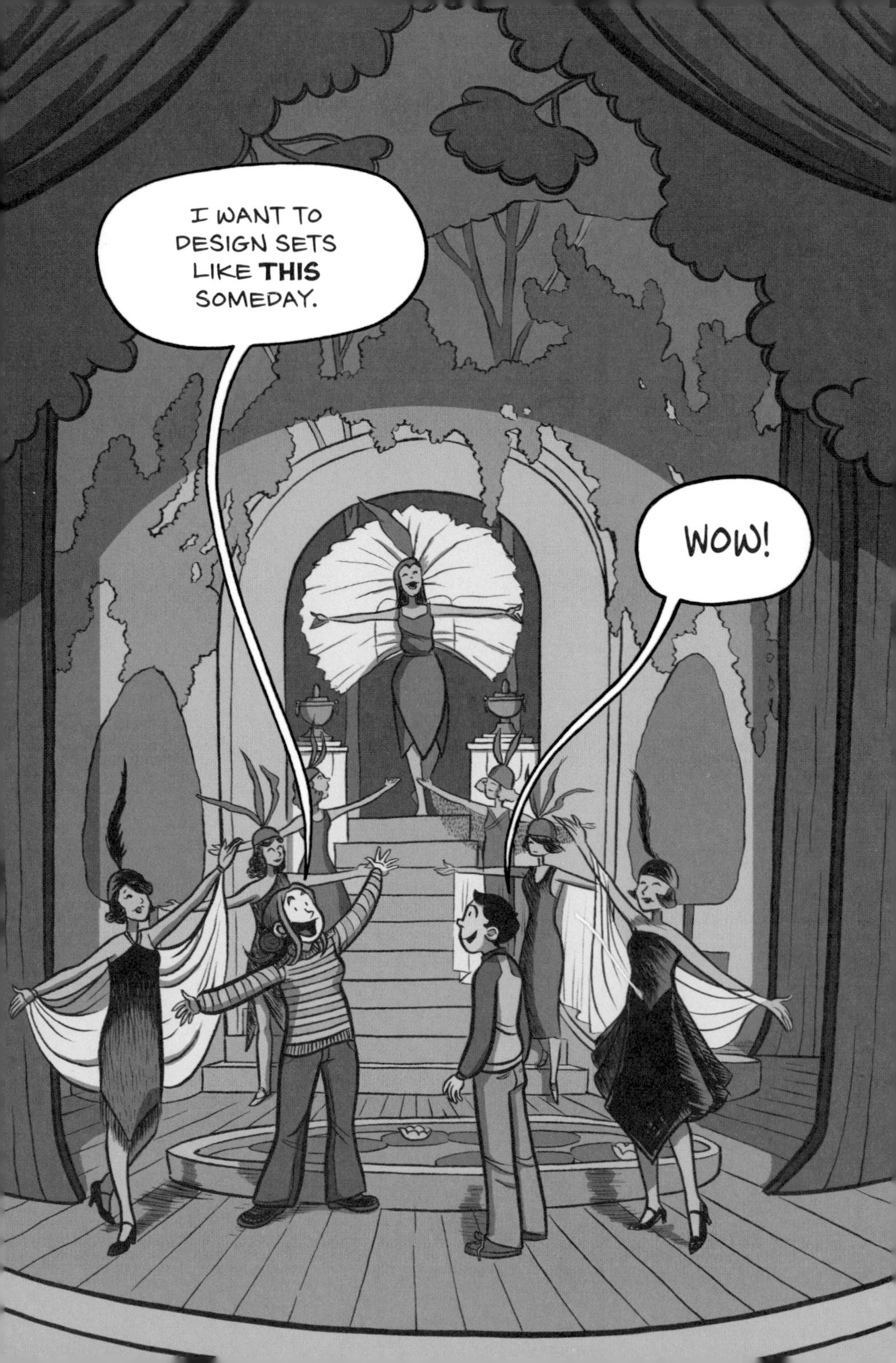
I WANT TO DESIGN SETS LIKE **THIS** SOMEDAY.
WOW!

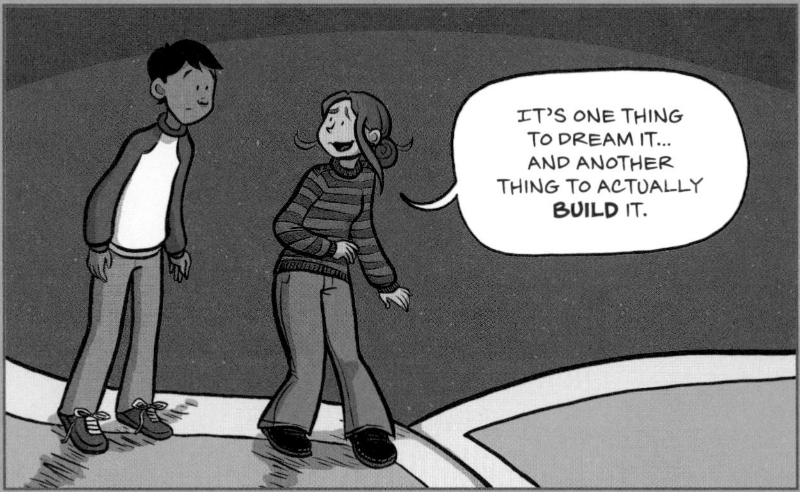
IT'S ONE THING
TO DREAM IT...
AND ANOTHER
THING TO ACTUALLY
BUILD IT.

STUDYING UP

A lot of research went into the creation of *Drama*. My friends and instructors in the theater, choir, and stage crew communities all contributed details that helped me bring the action of *Drama* to life. I may have participated in theater when I was in school, but I'm far from an expert! When I started developing *Drama*, I envisioned the main character, Callie, as being enamored with classic Broadway shows. The glitz and glamour of Old Hollywood-style theater are what make her tick, and in turn, I had to learn about those details, too.

Sometimes, you may have a great idea for a story, but the subject matter isn't something you're especially familiar with. And that's okay! The best way to develop a story idea based on a real topic is to research. Whether it's talking with experts, reading up on it in the library, or even going to museums and galleries, your job as an author is to uncover as many details as possible to give your story authenticity.

FIND YOUR SOURCE

Is there a subject that you'd like to write about but need to learn more before you start your story? Use these questions to prepare for an interview you might conduct with an expert on the topic you've chosen!

1. How long have you been involved with this subject?

2. What is your role in it?

3. What do you love about this subject? What drew you to it?

4. What are some of the most important things to know about your field of expertise?

5. What are some little-known details about this subject? Any insider information?

6. Can you share an interesting story about this subject? Either something unique about it or a unique personal experience?

7. If I were to write a story about this subject, what are some of the key elements to include?

8. If the characters in my story were involved in this subject, how might that influence the way they speak or act?

9. What would you suggest I read or study to learn more about this subject?

10. What resources helped you the most as you became an expert in your field?

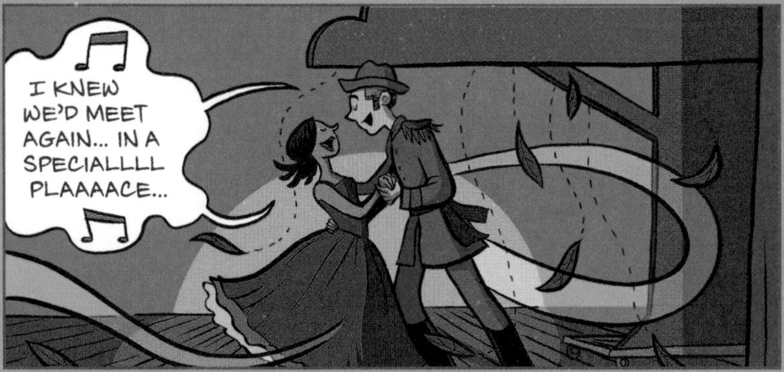
I KNEW WE'D MEET AGAIN... IN A SPECIALLLL PLAAAACE...

TELL YOUR SCHOOL STORY

Pencils out – it's writing time! Dig deep into your school experiences and choose some as inspiration. Think about your clubs, activities, classes, favorite school memories, and cringeworthy embarrassing moments, and come up with a concept that works for you. Try throwing in some unique elements that you're either an expert on or need to research in order to give your story depth. As for including any drama . . . that's up to you!

STORY IDEAS

Write out three different story ideas that you think would make a great school drama.

WRITE IT!

Choose one of your three ideas and write out the whole story.

STORY TITLE:

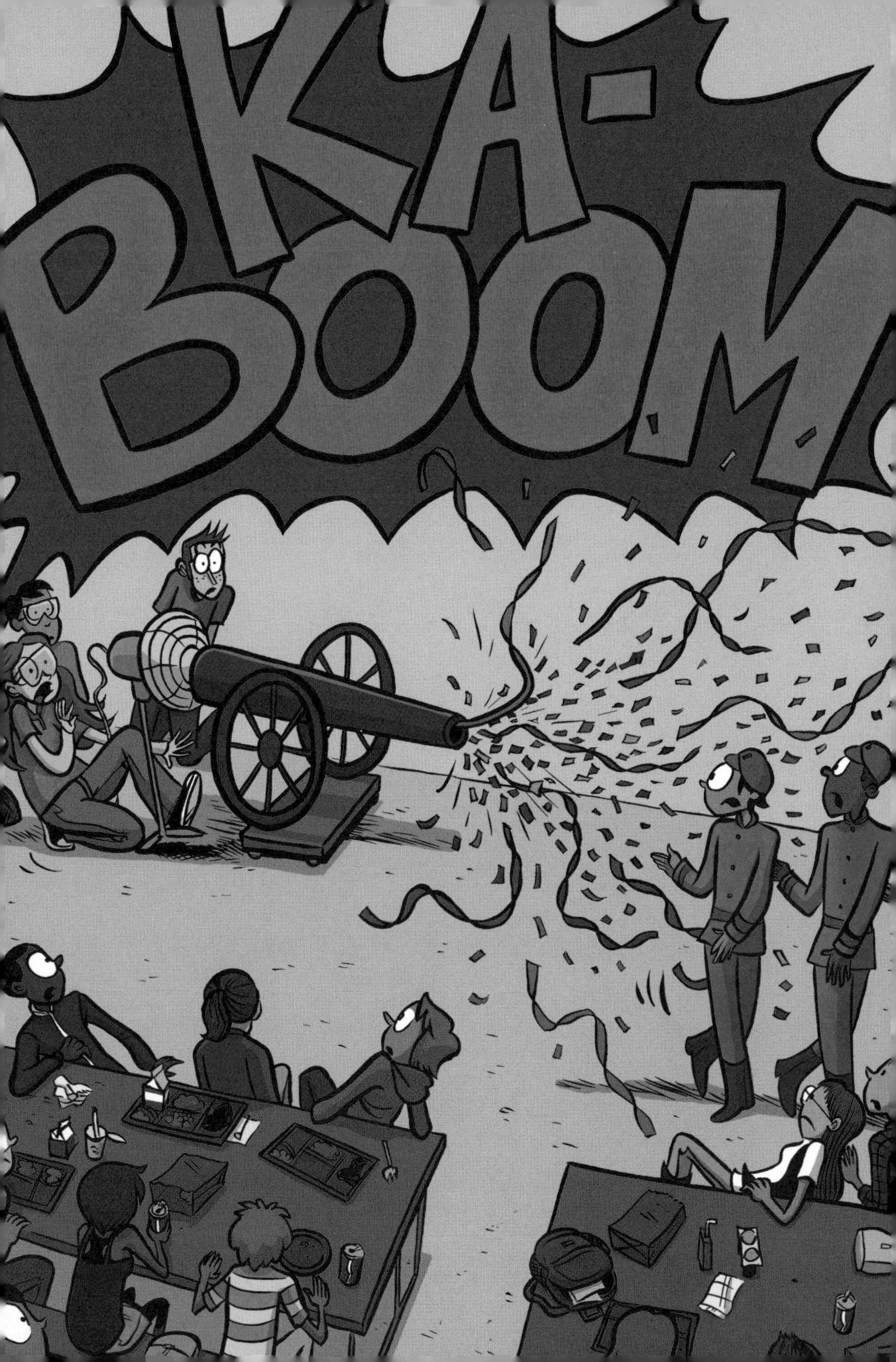
KA-BOOM!

Use the panels on these pages to draw the beginning of your story.
Don't forget to include word balloons!

CHAPTER 4
THE WORLD AROUND YOU

AN EXCERPT FROM *GHOSTS*

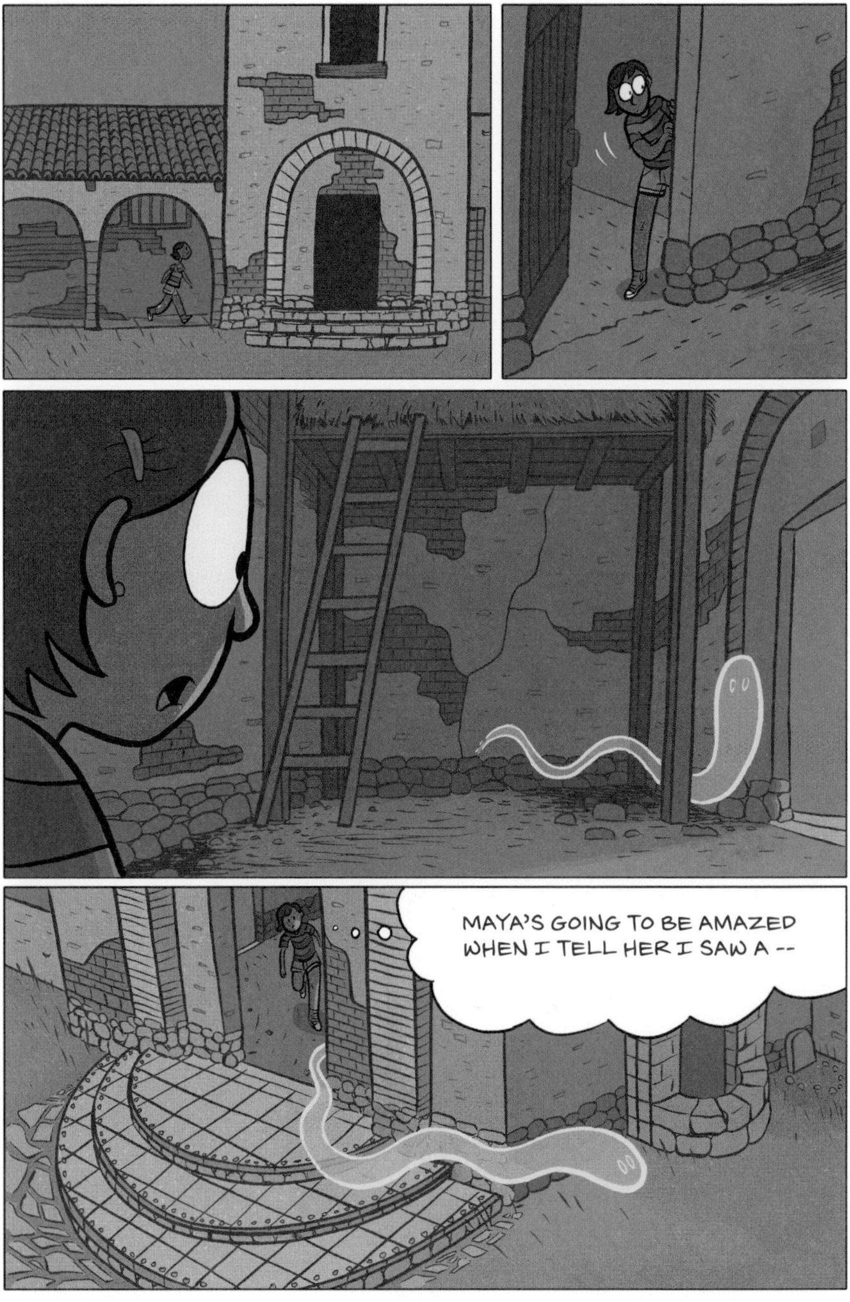
MAYA'S GOING TO BE AMAZED
WHEN I TELL HER I SAW A --

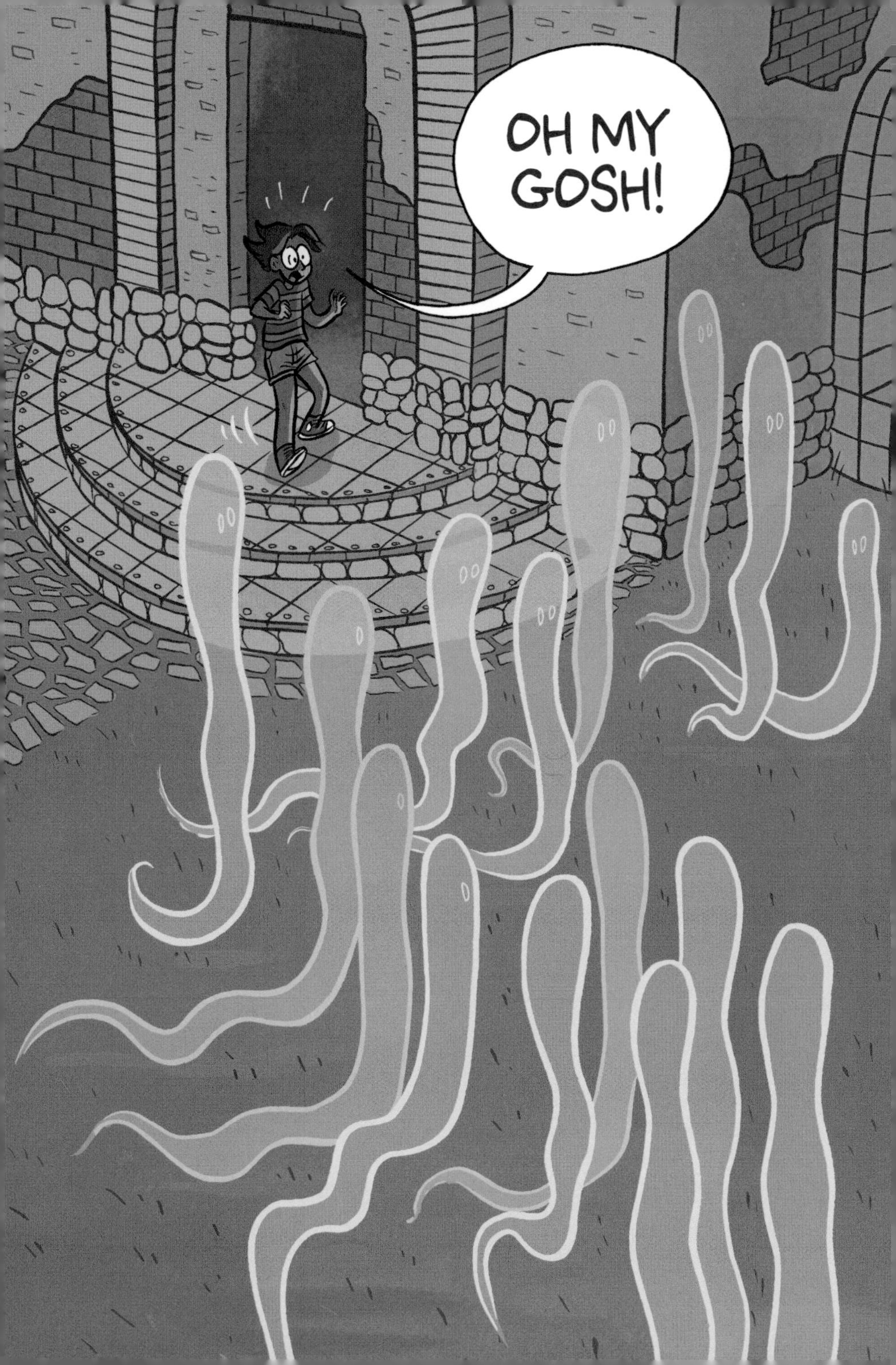
OH MY GOSH!

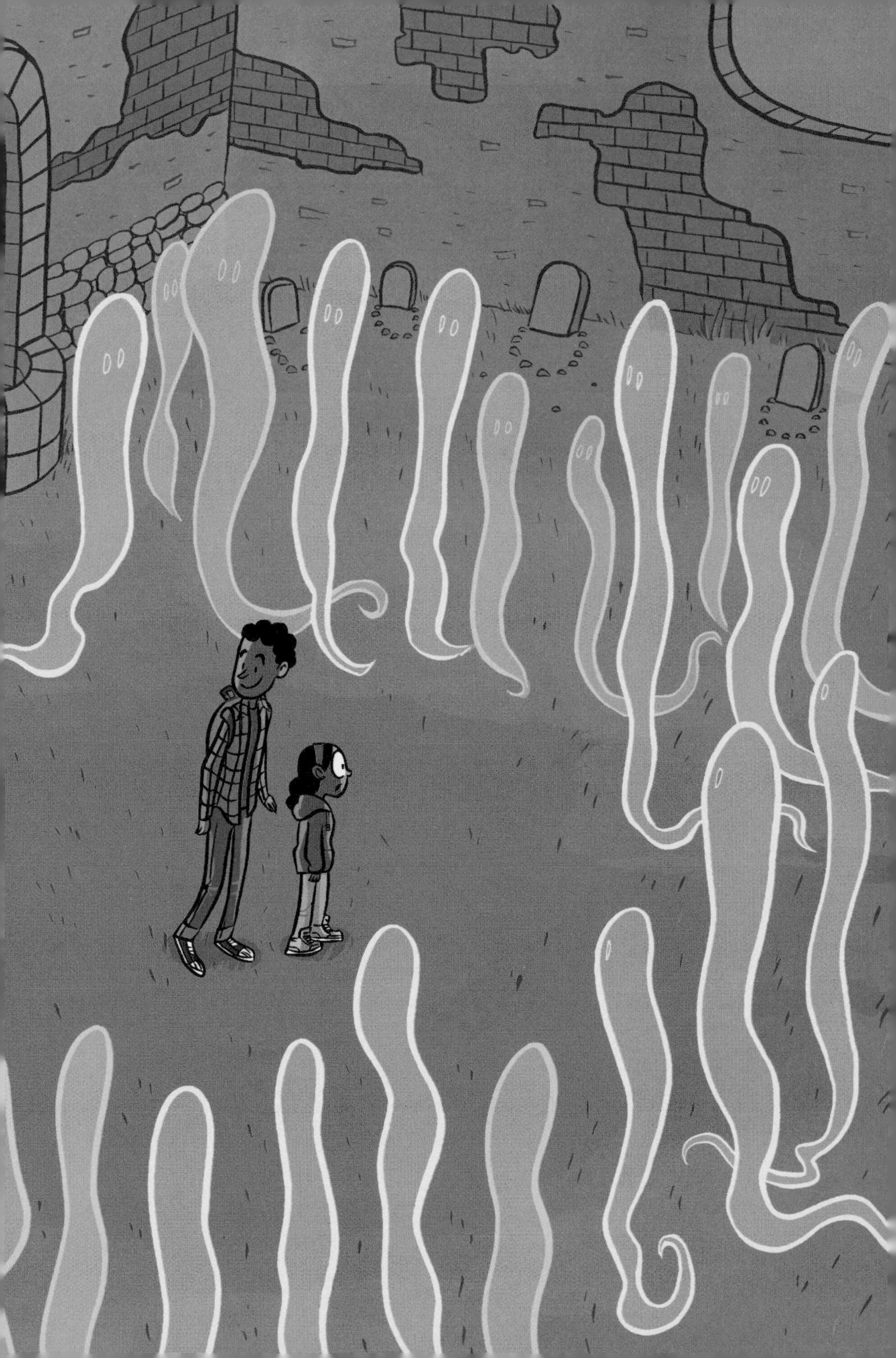

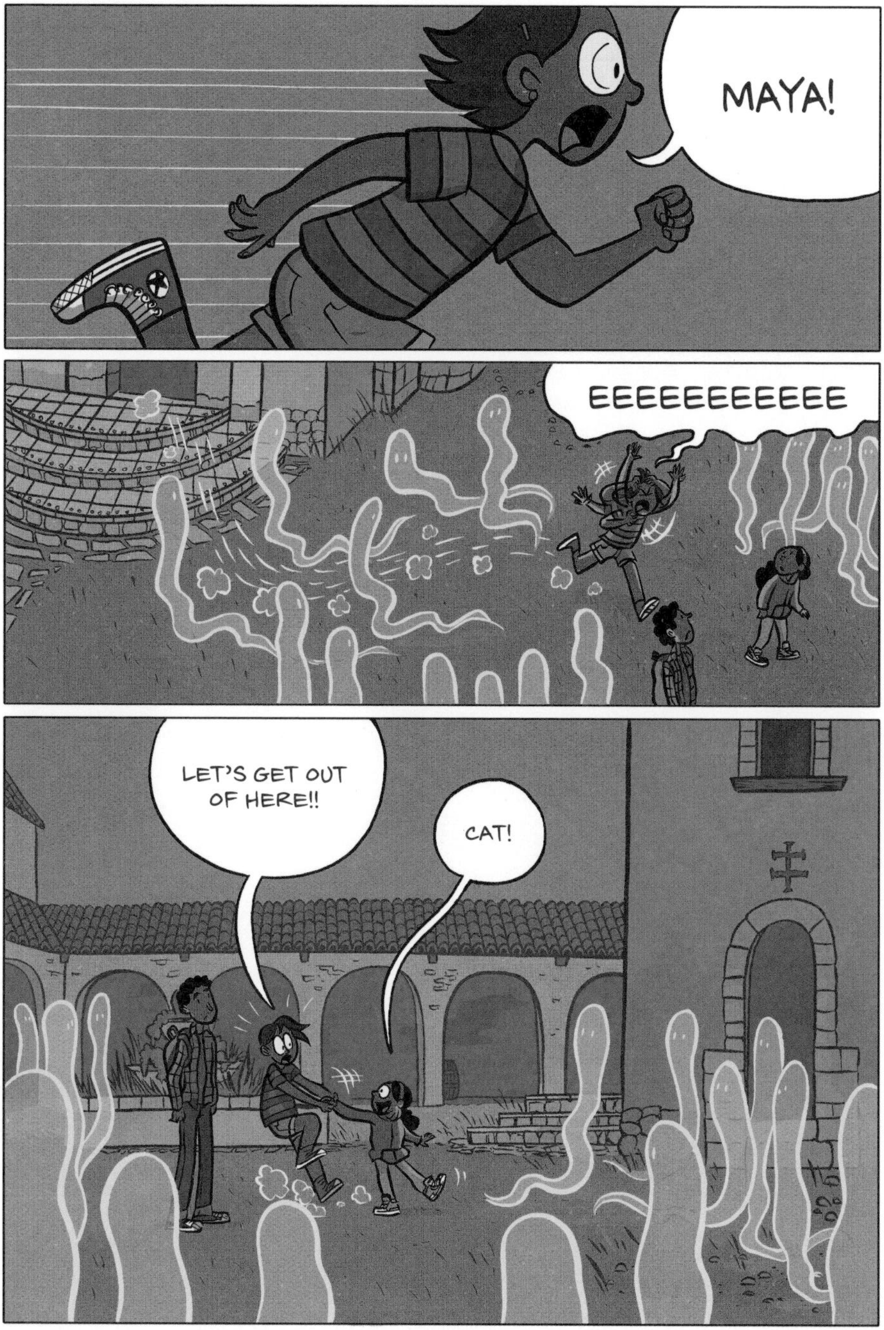
MAYA!
EEEEEEEEEEEE
LET'S GET OUT OF HERE!!
CAT!

CREATING ATMOSPHERE

A lot of great story ideas come from the way places make you feel. Some places can feel spooky and ethereal. Others can be calm, serene, and picture-perfect. These feelings might open up ideas you didn't know you had, because atmosphere can often influence your senses in a way that makes every experience unique.

I set my graphic novel *Ghosts* in a fictional coastal town called Bahía de la Luna. It was inspired by foggy Northern California, where I grew up. I've always had an appreciation for the windswept coastline, the gnarly cypress trees, and especially the seaside town of Half Moon Bay, which is famous for its artichoke fields, pumpkin farms, and cheerful, laid-back Halloween vibe. I wanted Bahía de la Luna to feel like that, and the characters who live there to reflect the slightly haunting atmosphere.

FROM RAINA'S SKETCHBOOK

These sketches were done in 2008, eight years before the publication of *Ghosts*!

ARTICHOKE ST.
CRESCENT BAY INN
VACANCY

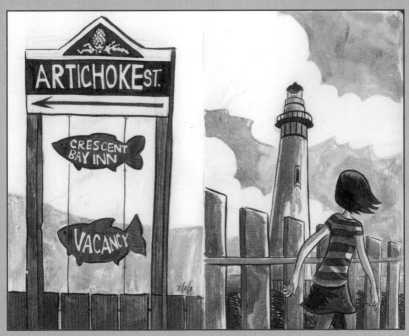

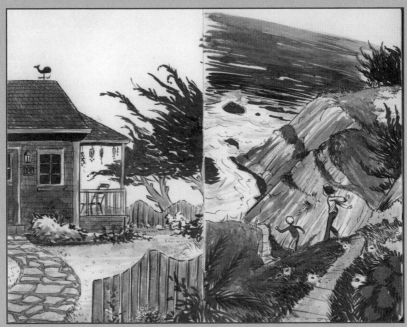

WHAT PLACES INSPIRE YOU?

Use these questions to unveil how the mysterious world around
you can help influence your next big story idea.

Use three words to describe what feelings the
following places evoke in you:

Tall mountains

A tropical island

The peaceful countryside

A big city

Endless ocean

A vast desert

Snow-covered hillsides

A wild jungle

What's one of the coolest places you've ever been?
What made it unique?

What is a place that is very special to you? Why?

How does your mood change when you go to different places?
Like school? A festival? Or someplace new you've never been before?

Describe the spookiest place you've ever visited.
Did anything strange happen there?

If you could invent a fictional town for your story, what would it
be like? How would the people there behave and interact?

GETTING INTO THE SPIRIT

Ghosts isn't just set in a town that feels slightly haunted. It actually is haunted! I was drawn to the idea of including supernatural elements while I was writing the story. The two main characters, sisters Cat and Maya, face very real-world problems: moving to a new town, grappling with Maya's cystic fibrosis, and learning to lean on family for support in an ever-changing world.

Northern California's atmospheric coastline inspired me to wonder: What if ghosts helped guide Cat and Maya on their journey? Though the sisters can't change the hard things they're facing, they can find hope from the kindred spirits of those who have traveled the path of life before them.

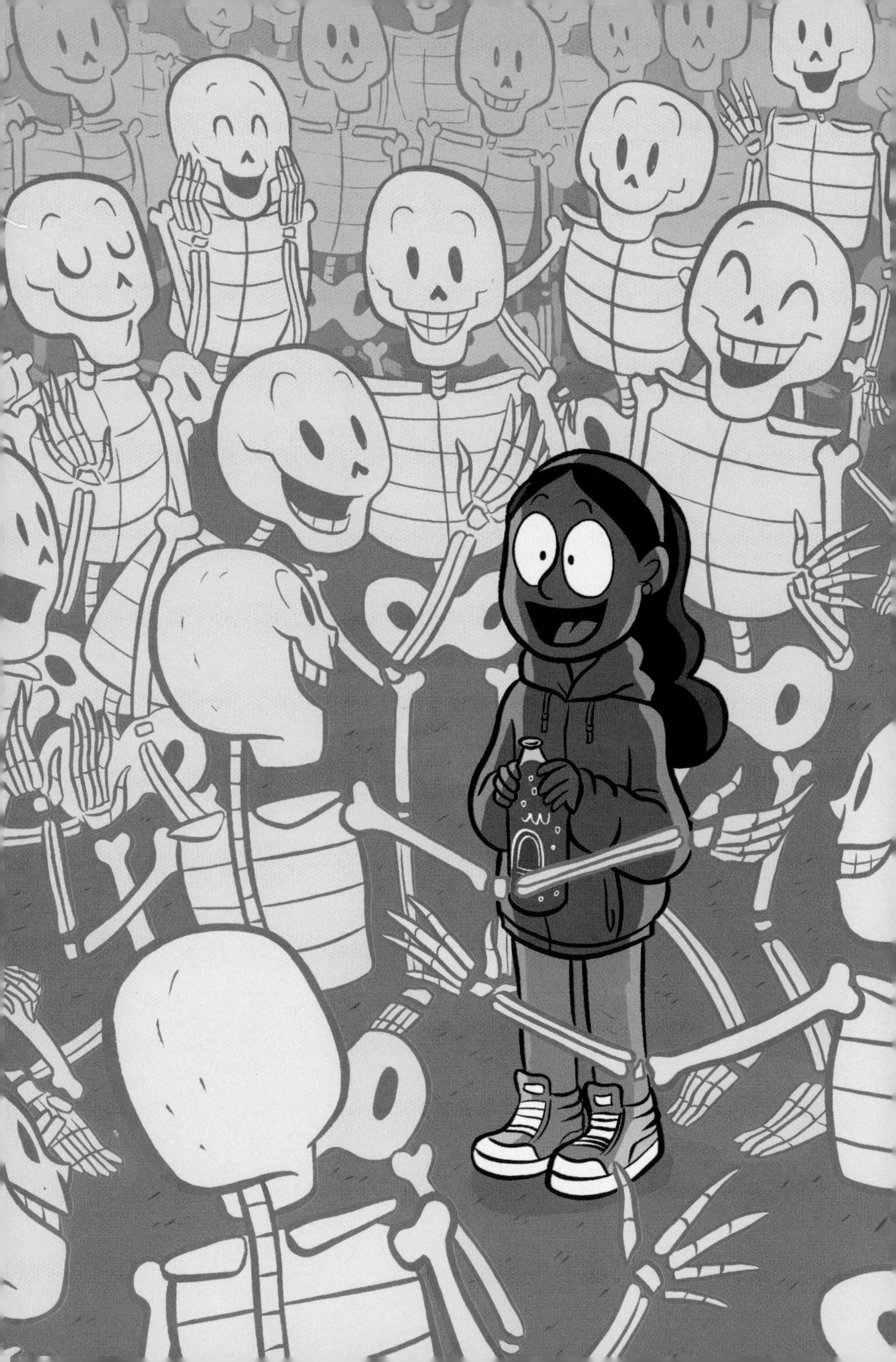

SEEKING THE SUPERNATURAL

If you were going to write a story with supernatural elements, what would they be? Keep in mind, there are lots of things that are supernatural - not just ghosts! Use these prompts to seek your next story's spooky side.

What supernatural being intrigues you? Why?

Have you ever been somewhere that was supposedly touched by the supernatural? How did it make you feel?

What's the spookiest story you've ever heard? How did it impact you?

How about the most inspirational or hopeful supernatural story you've ever heard?

Have you ever encountered something you felt was slightly . . . otherworldly? What happened?

Describe an out-of-this-world experience that would make a good story.

If you had to make up a supernatural character, what would they be like?

Draw a picture of your supernatural character here!

TELL YOUR OTHERWORLDLY STORY

In the spirit to write some more? Perfect! Try your hand at crafting a story using the feelings a unique place evokes in you, but with a supernatural twist.

STORY IDEAS

Write out three different story ideas that you think would make a great supernatural saga:

WRITE IT!

Choose one of your three ideas and write out the whole story.

STORY TITLE:

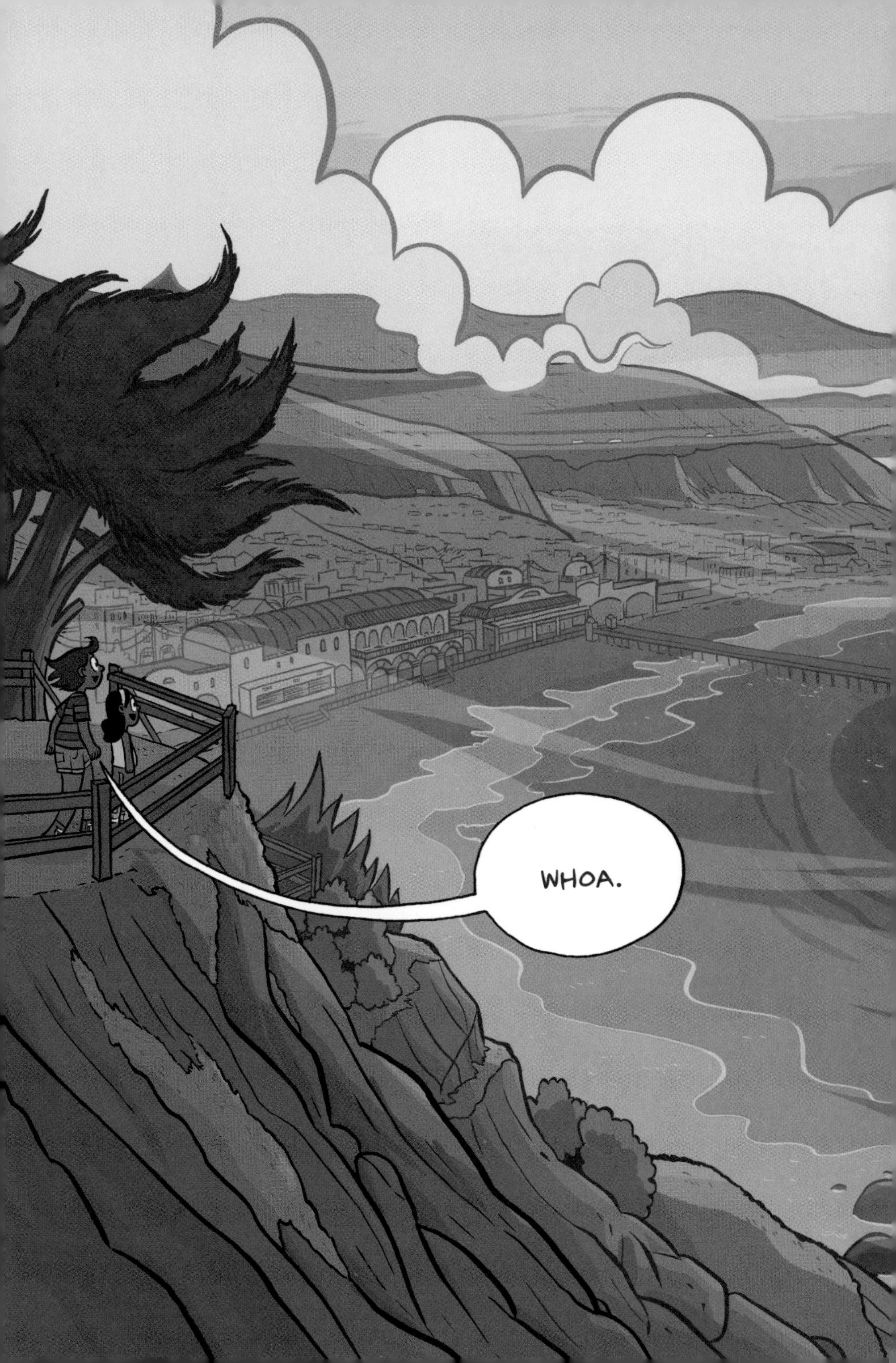
WHOA.

Use the panels on these pages to draw the opening to your story.
Don't forget to include word balloons!

KEEP SMILING

Great job! You're now well on your way to creating your own story, whether it's a memoir, fictional tale, or something completely new that could come only from you. Thanks for joining me on this journey. I hope learning a little bit about me has helped inspire you to kick-start your own storytelling career. It's a long road, but trust me, it's a great one. And if sharing our stories helps even one other person to smile, then it's all worth it in the end.

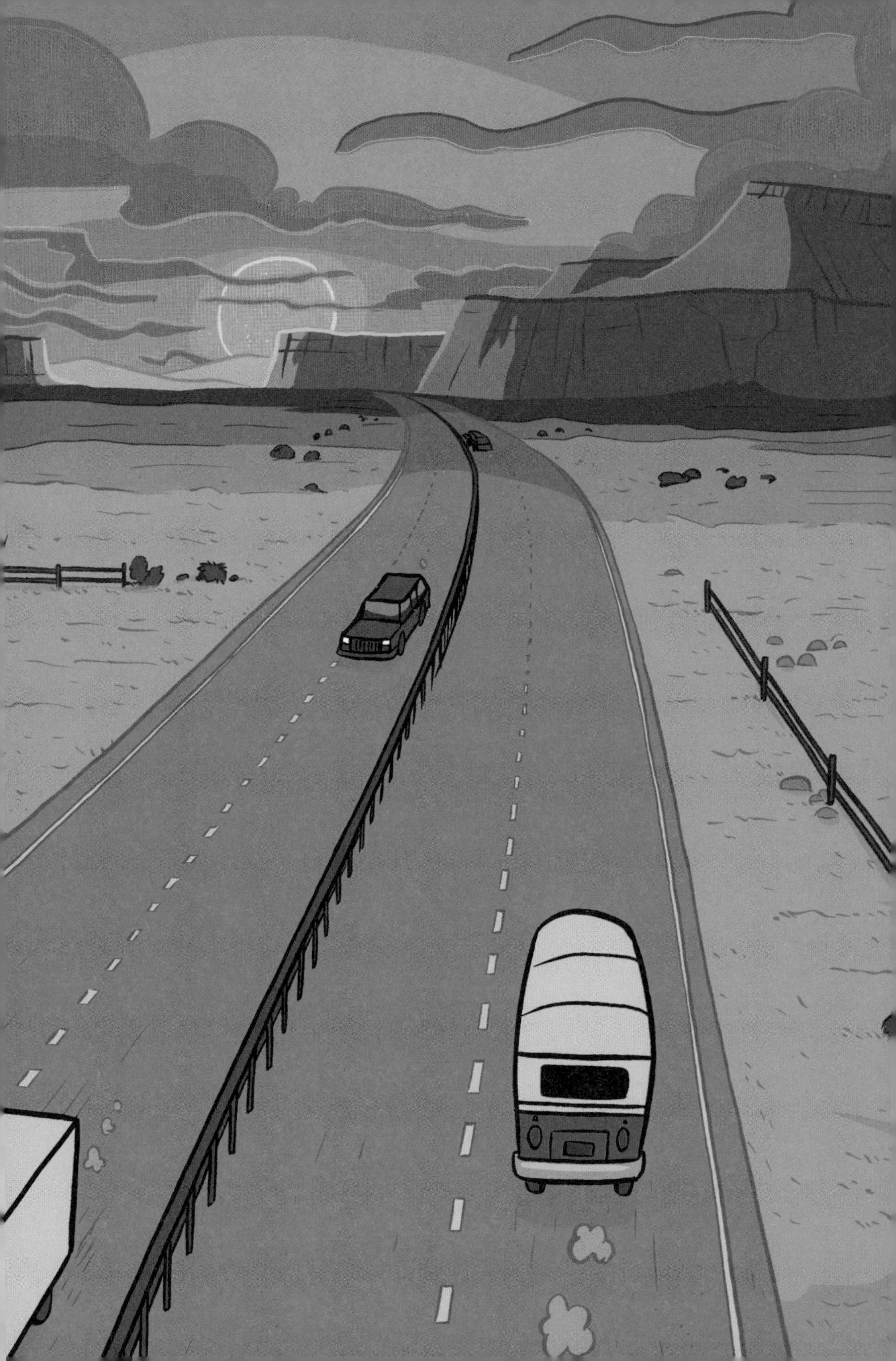

RAINA'S TIPS
FOR CREATIVITY

1. Keep a daily journal where you jot down notes for possible story ideas. You never know when inspiration will strike!

2. Practice sketching anything and everything, everywhere you go. The key to developing your artistic talent is to practice, practice, practice.

3. Join a writing club (or start your own!) where you and your friends share your writing and offer one another feedback. It's a great way to hone your craft and stay motivated.

4. Read – every day and diversely! The more types of writing you're exposed to, the more your worldview will expand.

5. Ask your English and art teachers for constructive criticism. They know your work best, after all.

6. Collaborate. Not everyone is the best artist. Not everyone is the best writer. But maybe you can do one and your friend can do another. Team up to create something!

7. Go to readings at your local bookstore or library to hear how other authors and illustrators got started. You could have a similar experience in the future.

8. It's okay to start small. Even if you have a big idea for an epic, multivolume series, you might find that it's easier to first try writing and drawing a short story based on your big idea.

9. Self-publish! Make copies of your pages, fold and staple them into booklets, and share them with your friends. You can absolutely call yourself a self-published author, because now you've made a minicomic!

10. Check out my website, goRaina.com, for even more writing and illustrating advice.

DON'T MISS RAINA'S
NEXT GRAPHIC NOVEL!

Raina once again brings us a true story from her childhood. From tummy aches and problems with friends to managing school bullies and surviving family chaos, Raina uses her signature warmth, charm, and humor to tell her story of growing up with anxiety and surviving the highs and lows of elementary school.

Keep reading for a special sneak peek!

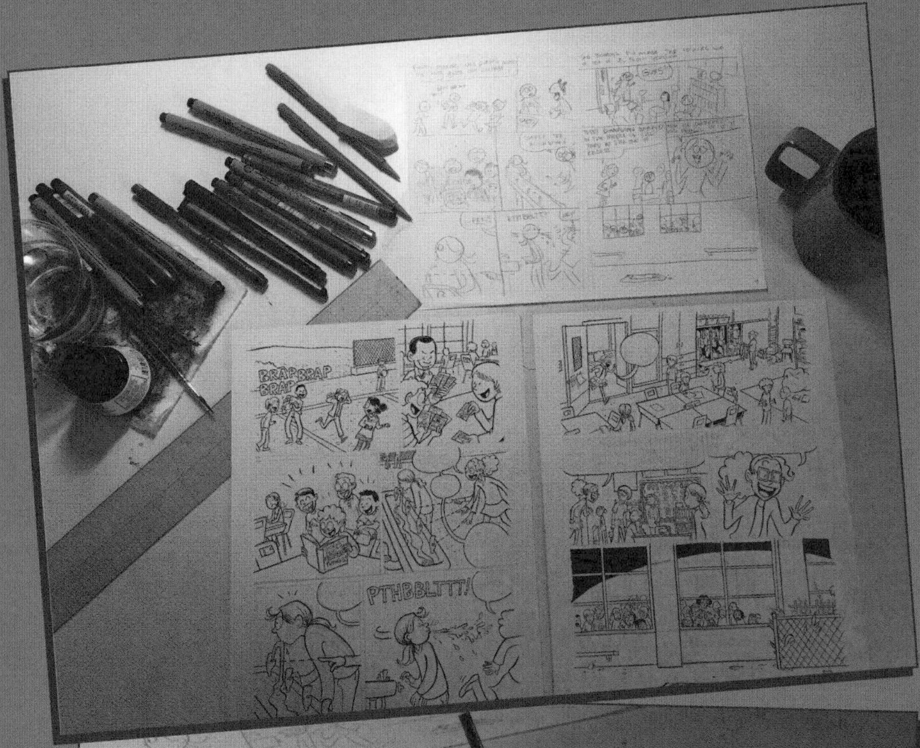
BRAPBRAP
BRAP
PTHBBLTTT!

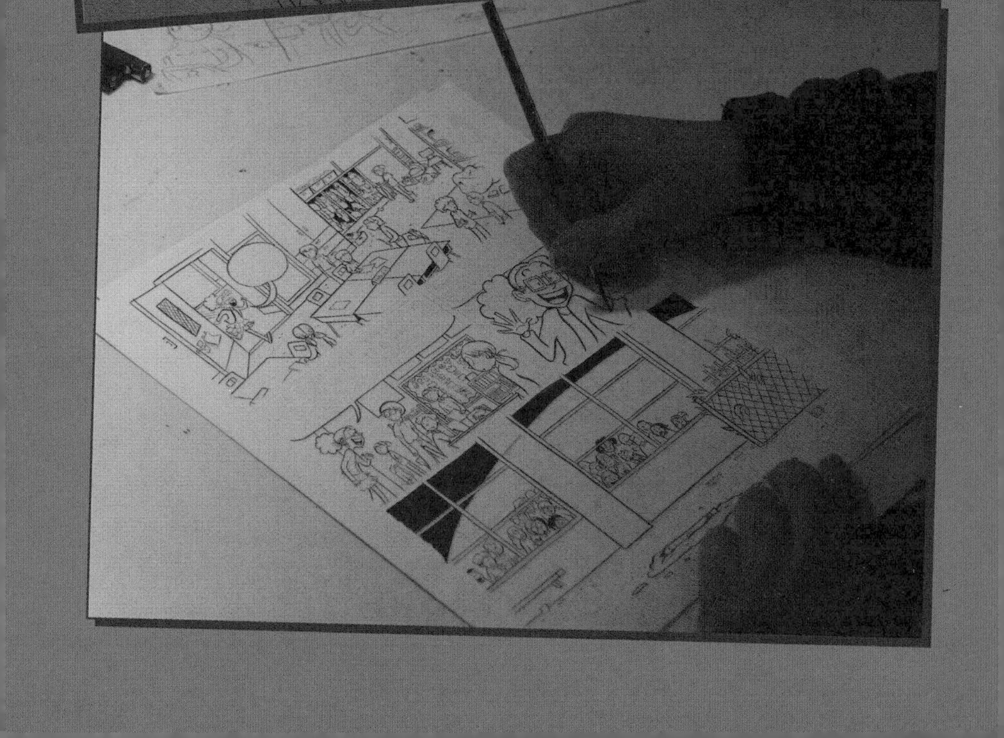

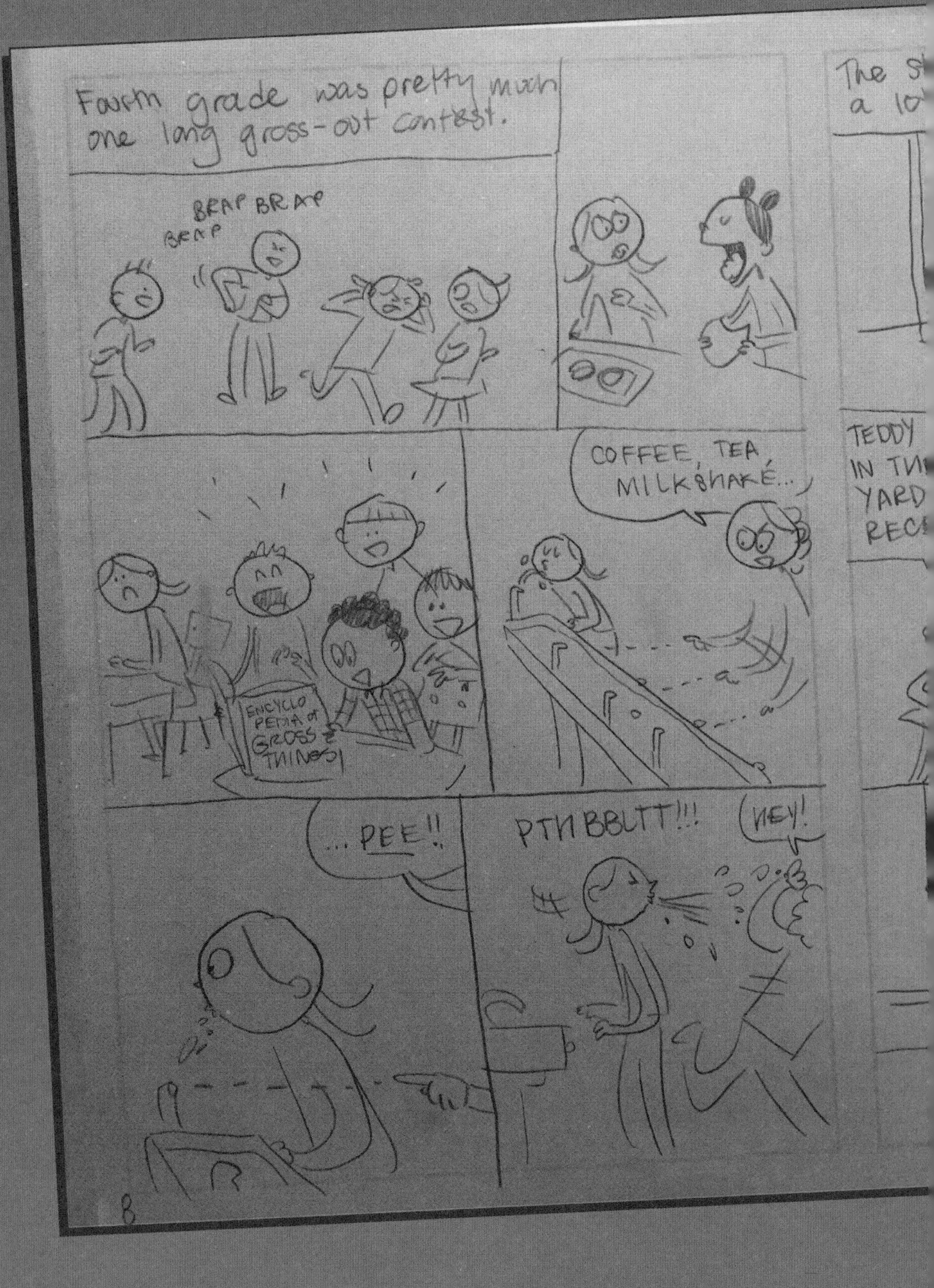
Fourth grade was pretty much one long gross-out contest.
BRAP BRAP
BRAP
ENCYCLOPEDIA of GROSS THINGS!
COFFEE, TEA, MILKSHAKE...
...PEE!!
PTHBBLTT!!!
HEY!
The s
a lo
TEDDY
IN TH
YARD
REC

Raina Telgemeier

Guts

I'm having so much fun working on my next book! I hope you enjoy these photos of my work in progress.

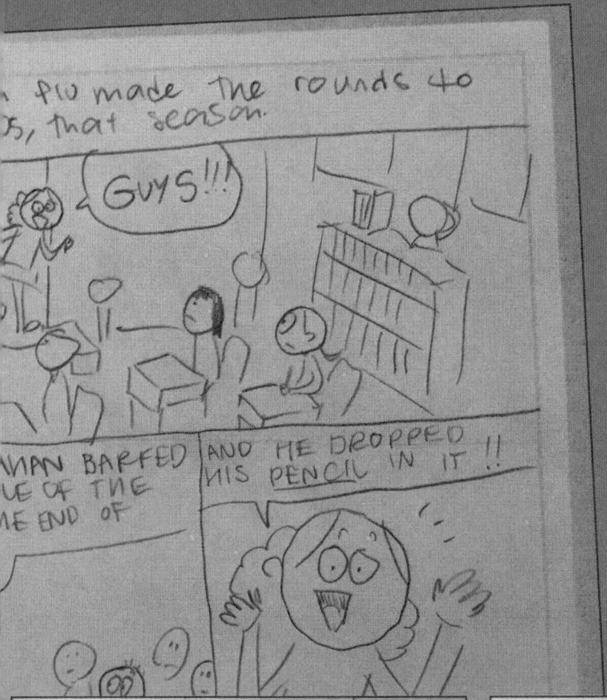
plu made the rounds to
that season.
GUYS!!!
AND HE DROPPED HIS PENCIL IN IT !!

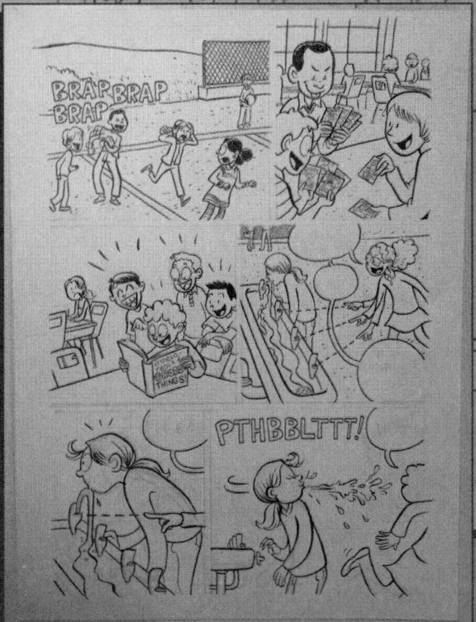
BRAP BRAP BRAP
PTHBBLTTT!

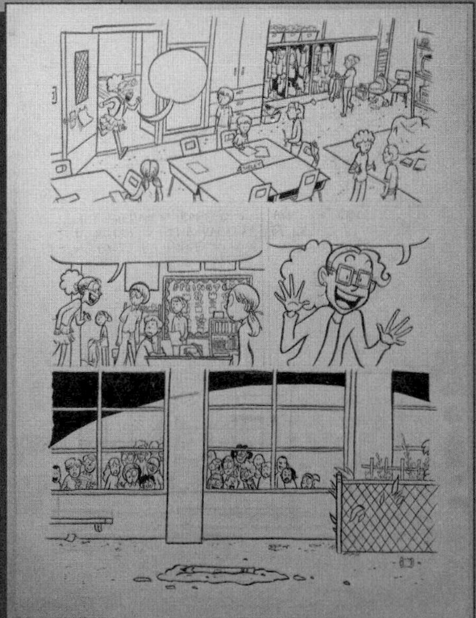

Keep reading to see what these pages will look like in the real book!

FOURTH GRADE WAS PRETTY MUCH ONE LONG GROSS-OUT CONTEST.

BRAP BRAP BRAP BRAP

COFFEE...

TEA...

MILK-SHAKE...

PEE!!

PTHBBLTTT!

HEY!

By Ann M. Martin and Raina Telgemeier

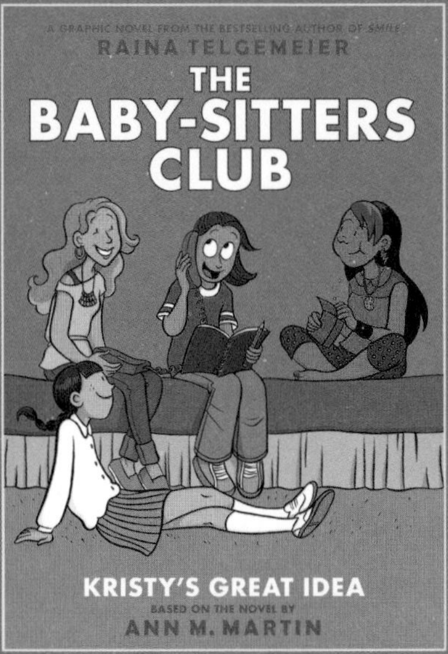
A GRAPHIC NOVEL FROM THE BESTSELLING AUTHOR OF *SMILE*
RAINA TELGEMEIER
THE BABY-SITTERS CLUB
KRISTY'S GREAT IDEA
BASED ON THE NOVEL BY
ANN M. MARTIN

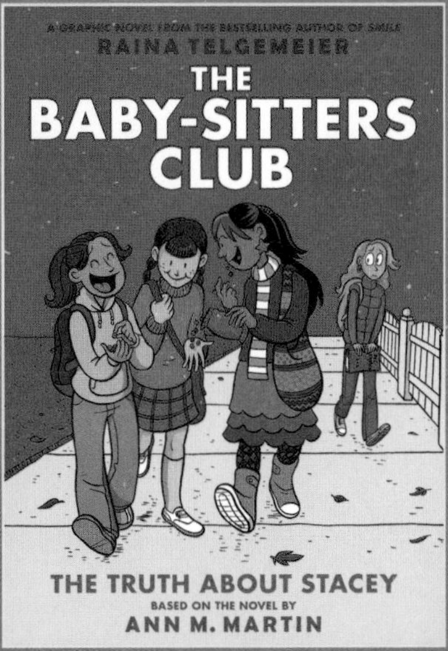
A GRAPHIC NOVEL FROM THE BESTSELLING AUTHOR OF *SMILE*
RAINA TELGEMEIER
THE BABY-SITTERS CLUB
THE TRUTH ABOUT STACEY
BASED ON THE NOVEL BY
ANN M. MARTIN

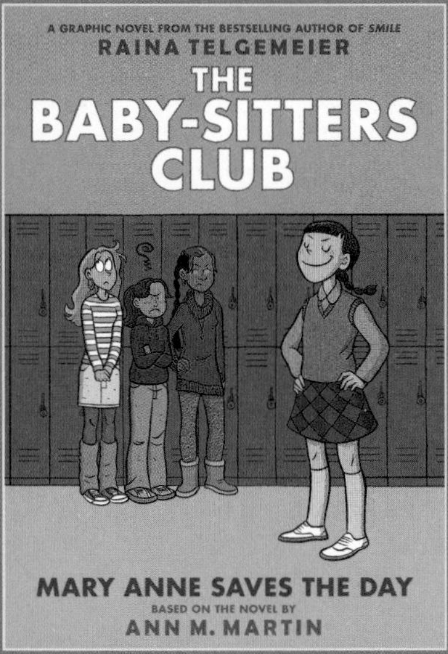
A GRAPHIC NOVEL FROM THE BESTSELLING AUTHOR OF *SMILE*
RAINA TELGEMEIER
THE BABY-SITTERS CLUB
MARY ANNE SAVES THE DAY
BASED ON THE NOVEL BY
ANN M. MARTIN

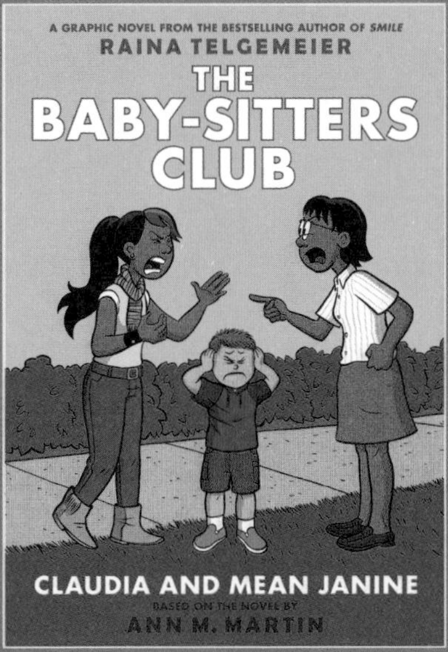
A GRAPHIC NOVEL FROM THE BESTSELLING AUTHOR OF *SMILE*
RAINA TELGEMEIER
THE BABY-SITTERS CLUB
CLAUDIA AND MEAN JANINE
BASED ON THE NOVEL BY
ANN M. MARTIN

Raina Telgemeier is the #1 *New York Times* bestselling, multiple Eisner Award-winning creator of *Smile* and *Sisters*, which are both graphic memoirs based on her childhood. She is also the creator of *Drama* and *Ghosts*, and is the adapter and illustrator of the first four Baby-sitters Club graphic novels. Raina lives in the San Francisco Bay Area. To learn more, visit her online at goRaina.com.

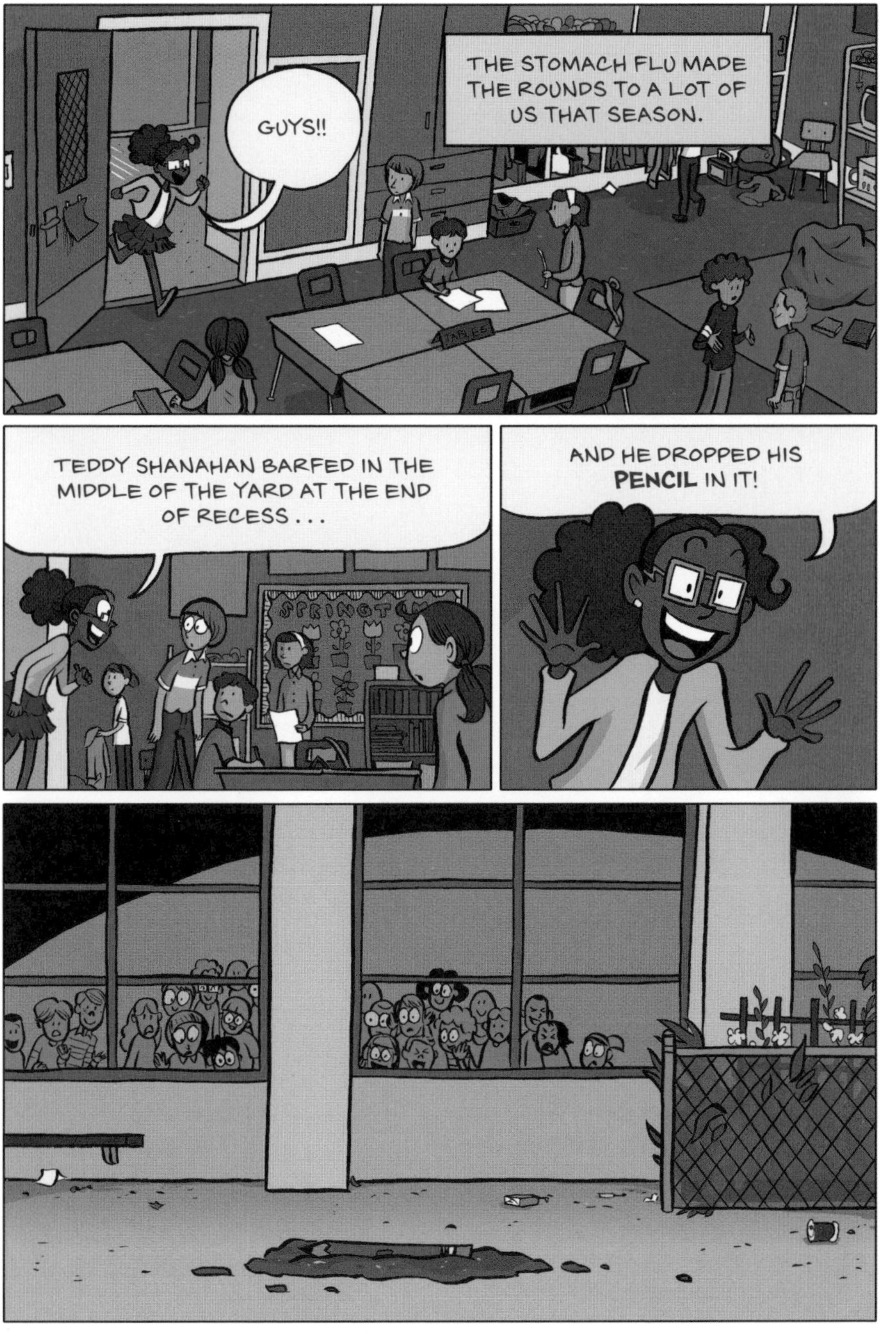
THE STOMACH FLU MADE THE ROUNDS TO A LOT OF US THAT SEASON.
GUYS!!
TEDDY SHANAHAN BARFED IN THE MIDDLE OF THE YARD AT THE END OF RECESS . . .
AND HE DROPPED HIS **PENCIL** IN IT!

Also by Raina Telgemeier

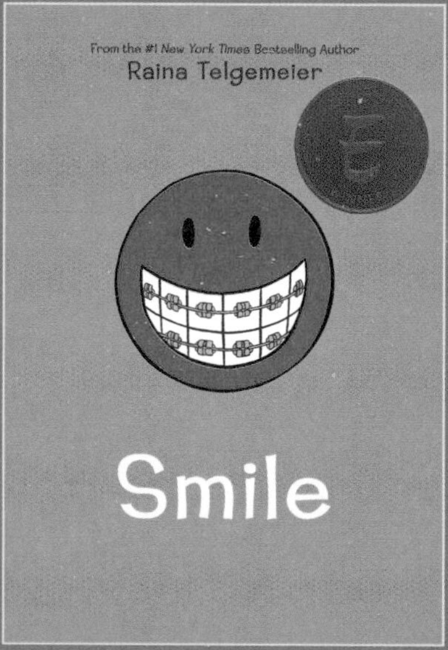
From the #1 New York Times Bestselling Author
Raina Telgemeier
Smile

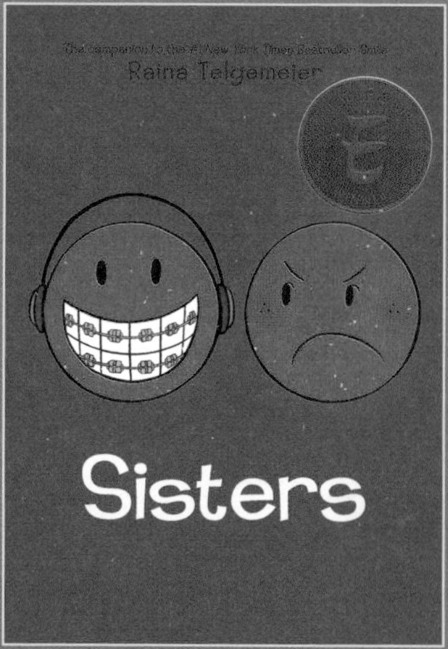
Raina Telgemeier
Sisters

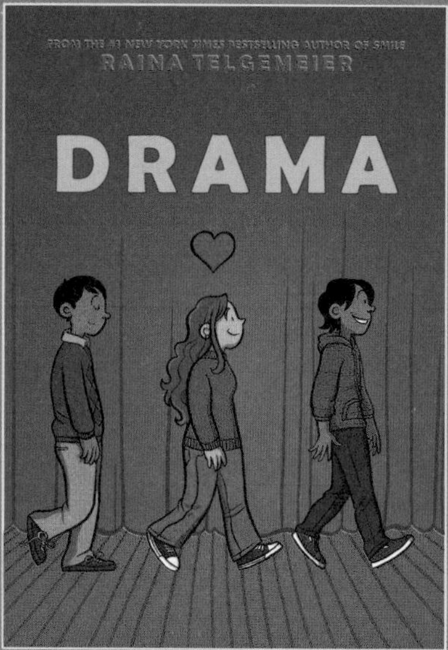
FROM THE #1 NEW YORK TIMES BESTSELLING AUTHOR OF SMILE
RAINA TELGEMEIER
DRAMA

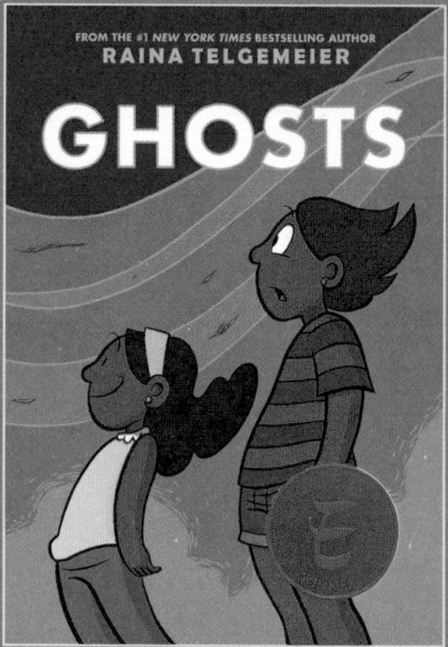
FROM THE #1 NEW YORK TIMES BESTSELLING AUTHOR
RAINA TELGEMEIER
GHOSTS